How You Remember Yesterday Determines
How You Will Live Tomorrow

The
GOD
MOMENT

Principle

ALAN D.
WRIGHT

Multnomah Publishers® *Sisters, Oregon*

THE GOD MOMENT PRINCIPLE
published by Multnomah Publishers, Inc.

© 1999 by Alan D. Wright
International Standard Book Number: 1-57673-579-6

Scripture quotations are from *The Holy Bible,* New International Version © 1973, 1984
by International Bible Society, used by permission of Zondervan Publishing House

Cover design and photography by
Kirk DouPonce

Back cover photograph by
David Olsen/Tony Stone Images

Multnomah is a trademark of Multnomah Publishers, Inc., and
is registered in the U.S. Patent and Trademark Office.

The colophon is a trademark of Multnomah Publishers, Inc.

Printed in the United States of America

For information:
MULTNOMAH PUBLISHERS, INC.
POST OFFICE BOX 1720
SISTERS, OREGON 97759

99 00 01 02 03 04 05 06 — 10 9 8 7 6 5 4 3 2 1

For Mary Budd,

My sister by marriage and by Jesus.

I knew you were a tender rose,
but I didn't know you were also a towering oak.
When I learned you were sick, I figured
I was here to help build your faith.
Now I know it was so you could build mine.

You are the real teacher.
I've been writing about the God Moment Principle,
but you've been living it—and with
such sweet fragrance and strength.

Oh, be well soon, Mary—our rose and our oak.

Be well soon—our tender, towering Mary.

Acknowledgments

My thanks to:

My beloved wife, Anne...these searing desert days would have made a common woman faint, but you have stood strong...no, you have walked far...no, you have flown high. These pages are precious, for their price was dear—and you were the one who covered the cost. It reminds me again of just how deep your riches run—in mercy, joy, peace, and love. I've seen God in you more than anyone on earth. You're my live-in God Moment.

Abigail, my only daughter, my darling...making you laugh by rubbing my nose on your tummy after your bath is my favorite part of the day. Your name means "my father is joyful," and with you in my arms now, he is.

Bennett, my only son, my best buddy...you said that when you grow up you want me to build you a house in the backyard so we can still play together every day. Oh, precious boy, I might...I just might.

Mom...how can I possibly tell of my love and gratitude? All of my God Moments are due to your prayers.

Jack...by loving my mother so, you love me; by loving God so, you lift me.

Dad...I would never wish these days of your sickness upon any family, but, strangely, I would not trade them. By the bed of your suffering, our souls have touched—and I have felt your love more deeply than ever before. Be well, Dad. I love you.

Graham and Bonnie, my parents-in-law...you are extraordinary givers. I cannot count the gifts you have given me—playtime with our children, trips to Disney World, support to Anne while I have been writing, sacrifice for whatever daughter has been hurting most. The highest blessing in my life was born from your marriage. My gratitude is beyond words and my love beyond my gratitude.

Stanley and JoElla Bennett...you live out the meaning of the Bennett name, blessing us all. Thanks for capturing our hearts with your God Moments. Seeing God in you makes us see God in us.

Linda Cooke...I'm not sure which amazes me more, that you make so few mistakes or that you put up with so many of mine. This year, more than any, you have had to read my mind, soothe my mind, and help me make up my mind. Other pastors drool when I tell them about my secretary.

The dream team, Reynolda staff...life's circumstances made me drop the ball a lot this year, but you were still slam-dunking it.

Reynolda Presbyterian Church...I love you immensely. Thanks for letting me tell the world some of your miracle stories.

Dan Benson, senior editor at Multnomah...scribbling notes on napkins at that Colorado Cracker Barrel was a highlight of my year. This book might not have happened if not for the sensitivity and gentleness of your character during its uncertain beginnings. You are more than an accomplished editor, you are an enduring friend.

Multnomah president, Don Jacobson...for long phone calls during your busiest times, for passionate leadership, but mostly, for letting me write this book.

Contents

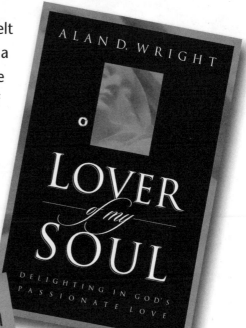

ALSO BY ALAN D. WRIGHT

Lover of My Soul

A Chance at Childhood Again

THE GOD MOMENTS OF YOUR LIFE

*I*t was one moment. But don't call it only a moment. Because that one moment transformed every other moment in James Cameron's life. It was transforming not just because of what it meant that day in 1930. It was life changing because one moment can live in a man's mind all the days of his life.

One moment that, through the awesome power of memory, he relives every day.

The emotions of the moment still beat with passion in his breast. He can still feel the sweat on his palms. He can still see the hate in their eyes. But mostly, he can still hear the sound of the Voice. It was life-changing because he knew it wasn't a lucky break, a fluke, or a figment of his imagination. He knew that on that day, and ever since, God was there. God made the moment.

The moment made the man.

James Cameron is a man whose life was made by a God Moment.

In Marion, Indiana, 1930, a furious mob of thousands held a beaten-but-innocent teenage boy in its trap. They held vengeance in their hearts. They held the law in their hands. They held the boy's neck in a noose. But, unknown to the crowd, God held the moment in His hands.

James Cameron was sixteen years old the night he rode around town with two friends. But Thomas Shipp and Abram Smith proved to be the wrong kind of friends. They convinced James to help them steal.

When the victim they planned to rob stepped from his car, James recognized him. James had shined the man's shoes regularly—a good customer. James forsook the wrongdoing and ran. Soon after, he heard gunshots. Later that night, James was arrested for the murder of his former customer and the rape of the victim's girlfriend.

While James was incarcerated with the two so-called friends, a furious mob assaulted the jailhouse. Unprotected by the sheriff, the innocent Cameron and his guilty friends were seized by the fuming crowd and beaten.

Then came the God Moment. Shipp and Smith were already gone—limp bodies hanging from the tree. Then the noose drew tight upon James Cameron's neck.

Imagine the terror of the moment. All is tense—the rope, the boy's muscles, the crowd's fists. Imagine the chaos of the moment. Everything is wild—the boy's heartbeat, the nooseman's eyes, the mob's imagination. Imagine the clamor of the moment. Everything is blaring—the curses, the cheers, the screaming.

What happened next in that Indiana town, only James Cameron knows for sure in his heart. And he does know it for sure. A sweet, undefiled, and distinct voice, unlike any he had ever heard, clearly called out: "TAKE THIS BOY BACK. HE HAD NOTHING TO DO WITH ANY RAPING OR KILLING."

More suddenly than it had begun, the chaos turned to calm. The tumultuous crowd tamed. The shouts quieted to silence. Mysteriously, the white crowd slowly parted, making room for the bewildered, beaten black boy to hobble back to the jail. Instead of hanging to death from the tree that day, Cameron was eventually given a fair trial and convicted of being an accessory before the fact to voluntary manslaughter. He served four years in prison.

*S*ome people say James Cameron imagined the voice. But Cameron knows that imaginary voices do not remove nooses from teenage necks. Some people say it was a human voice in the crowd. But Cameron knows that one mortal voice cannot quell the clamor of thousands. Some people say it was a lucky break. But Cameron knows that for black teenage boys accused of murdering a white man in 1930 there is no such thing as luck.

Today, the eighty-six-year-old Cameron says simply, "It was a voice from heaven. It was a miracle." If you ask him why it happened, he'll tell you confidently: "God saved me for [what] I'm doing today." Over the years, he has written books, spoken to crowds, and founded a museum. When asked if he had a choice between living a life in which the near-lynching happened and one in which it didn't, Cameron didn't hesitate: "I would rather have had it."[1]

Everyone would agree that James Cameron experienced a remarkable moment on that 1930 afternoon. No one could dispute the moment's importance. While his friends' bodies hung, Cameron's future hung. It was a life-and-death moment. But plenty of people have life-and-death moments. Narrow escapes. Near accidents. Close calls. James Cameron's experience was more than just an important moment in his life. It sculpted the shape of his destiny. It fueled the fire in his belly. It fed the gratitude of his soul.

Most people think that moments are just flashes in the pan—brief, fleeting events that are experienced and then evaporate. But moments are meant for more than that. Like the word's root, *movere,* "to move," pivotal moments are meant to move us. The Latin derivative, "momentum," is used in English as a physics term describing the product of a body's mass and velocity. Sports fans understand momentum to be the unseen force that turns the tide of a ball game. Likewise, moments are seemingly small movements which turn the scales of life. They can create history. They can shape the present and the future. But the moments must be apprehended for what they really are. They must be harnessed for what they really mean.

If James had assumed it to be a human voice in the crowd, he might have spent his life seeking a face to go with the voice. He would have been a grateful man with no one to thank. But he would not have developed a sense of destiny or purpose. If James had thought it was a fortunate fluke, he might have thanked his lucky stars. He might have spent his life hoping that some other lucky breaks would come along. But he would not have lived with a holy hope in his heart.

What changed James Cameron's life was knowing that not only was it an extraordinary moment, but also a supernatural moment. He knew God had spoken. In the middle of the most harrowing moment of his life, the boy heard God. So, for James, the event was not so much about the hatred of the crowd or the injustice of the times. It was about the love and purposes of God. Eternity invading time. Love diving into the midst of hate. Mystery interrupting mayhem.

Everyone has pivotal experiences of God's loving activity in their lives. I call them God Moments. You've had such moments. You may not have recognized God in the moments, but He's been there. Think about it.

Have you ever had a narrow escape from a tough situation by some strange protection? It probably was God who rescued you.

Have you ever steered away from trouble and toward something more noble because something inside you quietly craved purity? Only God makes people want to be clean.

Have you ever received a blessing that you know you didn't earn? God is the giver of all good gifts.

Have you ever made a good decision that took you in a surprisingly good direction just because you "felt led"? That was probably God speaking to you.

Have you ever gone through a hard time only to discover later that it prepared you for something greater in your life? God is good at bringing value out of adversity.

Imagine the blessing, power, and faith that would be released in your life if you could see God in the important moments of your past. I want

GOD MOMENTS MEMO

FIVE KINDS OF GOD MOMENTS

1. **Amazing Rescue**—a moment when God guarded you, healed you, rescued you, or made a way out for you
2. **Holy Attraction**—a moment when God led you toward a healthier path, enabled you to resist a temptation, or inspired you to take the high road
3. **Unearned Blessing**—a moment when God gave you an unexpected blessing or an undeserved gift
4. **Revealed Truth**—a moment when God spoke to you through the Bible, inner peace, wise counsel, or a God-inspired message
5. **Valuable Adversity**—a moment in which God sustained you in a difficult time or made you stronger through the test of adversity

to help you discover your God Moments and help you weave them into the fabric of your daily life.

James Cameron not only recognized that it was God who acted in the moment, he also decided that he would never forget it. He's eighty-six years old, and he's appearing this week at a local university to speak about his experience. He'll be signing copies of his book that tells the story. He's never stopped thinking about the moment God spoke. He rehearses it in his mind over and over, and he's never stopped telling others.

I'm convinced that God has been involved in your life just as powerfully as he has been in James Cameron's. Your life is full of God Moments! The difference between James Cameron and most people is not that he had a special moment of divine intervention; the difference is what he did with the moment. The question is not whether you have had God Moments; the question is, have you harnessed their life-changing power?

*R*ecently, I was overwhelmed by a passage of Scripture that I had previously read dozens of times. You've probably read it many times too. But suddenly, the text exploded with power. A neglected but infinitely powerful biblical principle leaped from the page and into my heart.

The excerpt follows the story of the Exodus in which God brought His people out of their slavery in Egypt. After God "passed over" the homes of the Hebrews who had sprinkled blood on their doorposts, He gave a command through His servant Moses. I had always focused my study and preaching on the drama of the deliverance of the captive Israelites and the suspense of the evil Pharaoh's pursuit. But suddenly I realized that, in the midst of this sweeping story, there's a gigantic secret for abundant life: "Commemorate this day, the day you came out of Egypt, out of the land of slavery, because the Lord brought you out of it with a mighty hand." Moses continues with the Lord's command: "For seven days eat bread made without yeast and on the seventh day hold a festival to the Lord" (Exodus 13:3, 6). The leader of Israel then gives God's clear reasoning:

> This observance will be for you like a sign on your hand and a
> reminder on your forehead.... For the Lord brought you out of

Egypt with his mighty hand. You must keep this ordinance at the appointed time year after year. (Exodus 13:9–10)

"Commemorate." It means making a planned effort to remember. Rehearse it. Take practical steps to make sure you don't forget it. *"A reminder...."* The whole reason for the festival (and all the appointed feasts of Israel) was to help God's people remember. The simple command to remember pervades the pages of the Old Testament:

"Do not forget the things your eyes have seen or let them slip from your heart" (Deuteronomy 4:9, emphasis added).

"Remember that you were slaves in Egypt and that the Lord your God brought you out of there with a mighty hand and an outstretched arm" (Deuteronomy 5:15, emphasis added).

"Remember how the Lord your God led you all the way in the desert these forty years, to humble you" (Deuteronomy 8:2, emphasis added).

"Remember the Lord your God, for it is he who gives you the ability to produce wealth" (Deuteronomy 8:18, emphasis added).

"I will *remember* your miracles of long ago. I will meditate on all your works" (Psalm 77:11–12, emphasis added).

"Forget not all his benefits" (Psalm 103:2, emphasis added).

"Don't be afraid of them. *Remember* the Lord" (Nehemiah 4:14, emphasis added).

"Remember the LORD in a distant land" (Jeremiah 51:50, emphasis added).

(See also Exodus 20:8; Deuteronomy 9:7; 15:15; 16:12; 32:7; Psalm 42:6; 105:5; 143:5; Isaiah 46:8–9; Zechariah 10:9.)

The powerful principle of remembering God Moments continues in the New Testament:

"Don't you *remember* the five loaves for the five thousand?" (Matthew 16:9, emphasis added).

"I will always *remind* you of these things.... I think it is right to refresh your memory" (2 Peter 1:12, emphasis added).

"You have forsaken your first love. *Remember* the height from which you have fallen!" (Revelation 2:4–5, emphasis added).

Remember. Remember. Remember. Arguably, it is the most basic command of Scripture. Almost every book of the Bible alludes to the importance and power of memory. The Hebrew word for "male," *zacha,* comes from the word for memory, *zachor.* To be a real man, in God's eyes, is to remember well.

*N*o one wants God's people to remember His miracles more than God Himself. The Lord didn't want it to be difficult for us to remember all He has done—He wanted to make it as simple as possible. So God gave His people a specific tool for harnessing the power of their moments with the Lord. God appointed seven festivals throughout the year that all Israel was required to celebrate. Each festival was designed to foster the memory of specific God Moments. If rightly celebrated by the Hebrews, the detailed festivals would virtually insure that God's people would remember His hand in their lives—for all of their lives.

Christians, of course, are not restricted by the specific Mosaic laws. Paul clearly explains to the Colossian Christians: "Therefore do not let anyone judge you by what you eat or drink, or with regard to a religious festival, a New Moon celebration or a Sabbath day. These are a shadow of the things that were to come; the reality, however, is found in Christ." (Colossians 2:16–17). The duties of the feasts are not incumbent upon the Christian, but the dynamics of them are. Christians are not bound by the proscription of the festivals, but we are empowered by their principles. With all the Old Testament underpinning, it is not surprising that Jesus' culminating moment with the disciples hinges on the memory command: "Do this in remembrance of me."

The modern evangelical church has been edified by excellent teaching about such principles as the power of praise, the gift of the blessing, and experiencing God. But we have neglected perhaps the greatest biblical principle for faith: remembering God Moments. Remembering yesterday's God Moments builds your faith for tomorrow's tests.

The way you remember yesterday determines how you will live tomorrow.

Even mature, well-meaning Christians have an incredible ability to forget extraordinarily beautiful moments of God. The memory dulls. The moment loses its luster. And soon, its life-changing power is gone.

But for the one who doesn't forget, there unfolds a glorious destiny. Consider more than James Cameron's story. Consider the faith heroes of God's Word...

- Noah...who hauled cypress wood, hammered planks, and gathered animals when there wasn't a cloud in the sky just because he remembered the day God spoke to him;
- Abraham...who raised a knife above the taut neck of his son on the altar, knowing God would provide the sacrificial ram because he remembered the day his elderly wife gave birth to the boy God had promised;
- Joseph...who graciously forgave the brothers who betrayed him because he remembered it was God who had given him the dream and appointed him ruler of Egypt;
- Joshua...who marched around the Jericho walls on Day Seven believing stone fortresses can be penetrated without a ladder or battering ram because he remembered how they crossed the Jordan waters without a bridge or a boat;
- David...who ran toward the giant rather than away from him because he remembered how God had strengthened him before, saying, "The Lord who delivered me from the paw of the lion and the paw of the bear will deliver me from the hand of this Philistine" (1 Samuel 17:37);
- Paul...who never forgot the blinding light or the striking voice that spoke to him outside Damascus but repeated it everywhere—even to King Agrippa—saying: "I was not disobedient to the vision" (Acts 26:19);
- Jesus...who was tempted in the desert but remembered the Word of God
  ...who bled in the garden, but remembered the reason for His coming
  ...who hung on the cross, but remembered the glory of Paradise
  ...who broke bread and commanded, "Do this in remembrance of me."

*J*ames Cameron had a moment that changed him forever. You probably have had similar moments that you discounted as coincidence, luck, or fluke. You may have celebrated some God Moments briefly and then lost them in the fog of daily stress. I want to help you find those priceless moments so you can celebrate them again. I'll help you start your treasure hunt by pointing you toward the five major kinds of God Moments. I'll offer some practical help so you can then harness the power of the God Moments you uncover. I'll show you how to mark your moments with God, like the Israelites did with stone pillars, to help you never forget your encounters with the Almighty. But, mostly, I want these pages to fill your heart with fresh joy and faith.

If you don't believe God has been in your life, please join me on this journey. You are in for more than an eye-opener. You're in for a life-changer. If you've always believed that God is working in you, walk with me. You are in for more than a memory-refresher. You're in for a faith-builder. If you're in a current struggle, stay close. There's real hope ahead. The God Moment Principle has immeasurable potential for your life. I won't promise you a magical end to all your problems. I dare not promise you perfect peace, health, or wealth. But I am confident of this: Other than the Word of God itself and the power of the Holy Spirit, the God Moment Principle is the single most powerful tool for faith in the universe.

"It is a delightful and profitable occupation to mark the hand of God in the lives of ancient saints, and to observe His goodness in delivering them, His mercy in pardoning them, and His faithfulness in keeping His covenant with them. But would it not be even more interesting and profitable for us to remark the hand of God in our own lives? Ought we not to look upon our own history as being at least as full of God, as full of His goodness and of His truth, as much a proof of His faithfulness and veracity, as the lives of any of the saints who have gone before? ...Let us review our own lives. Surely in these we may discover some happy incidents, refreshing to ourselves and glorifying to our God."[2] —CHARLES H. SPURGEON

CHAPTER ONE

THE FAITH-BUILDING POWER OF GOD MOMENTS

*I*t's late. My two happy children are finally in bed. They don't know that their mother was broken by the broken world tonight. They didn't see her tears. They don't know that their preacher dad stole away to the bedroom, closed the door, wiped a tear, and tried preaching to himself.

Thankfully, they're so young and resilient that they'll not be undone by the fact that this was the season we were supposed to take the long-awaited Disney World trip. But their granddaddy canceled the reservations a couple of weeks ago. My little girl's just a baby. All she knows is that Daddy hasn't been holding her as much lately. My boy's four. All he knows is that Auntie Mary is sick and that Gramps is in the hospital.

They don't know that my wife's thirty-three-year-old sister, Mary, has been told she has a two-inch carcinoma in her lung that has metastasized throughout her bones. When we found out, Anne simply said, "She's not just my sister, she's my best friend." It's true. Mary and her husband, Joe, have four children. Their children play with ours every day.

I think I love Mary enough to trade places with her. But I can't. Instead, they need me to be a man of prayer and faith. They need a look of confidence on my face that says, "God is on His throne and we are in His hands." In my own house, my wife needs not only a compassionate mate, but also a hopeful husband. Where do I find the faith?

My four-year-old knows that Gramps is in the hospital here in our hometown. He doesn't know that his grandfather has become completely disoriented—unable to walk, eat by himself, talk coherently, or hold his head upright. That's my daddy. He's always been a brilliant communicator. But now, at only age sixty-four, doctors don't know if I'll ever have a real conversation with him again.

This coming Sunday, a crowd of saints will be waiting for a word of passionate proclamation from my pulpit that God is good—all the time. Given the dryness of my current desert, where will I find living water for my own soul and for the thirsting crowds? What light is there in the valley of the shadow of death?

When life gets tough and joy wears thin, what do you do?

HOW REAL FAITH IS FORGED

For all of my Christian years, I've heard preachers, counselors, and friends answer that question this way: *Have more faith.* I know what they mean. They mean, *Don't worry. Just trust God and believe His promises.* It's good advice. In fact, I've been doling out that very exhortation for over a decade. It's biblical. Faith moves mountains and God loves faith. The Bible clearly tells us that without faith it is impossible to please the Lord (Hebrews 11:6).

Right now, however, if you tell me things like "Have faith" and "Don't worry, God's in control," I'll appreciate your effort but it won't help me much. I *want* more faith. But *telling* me to have more faith doesn't give me more faith. In fact, sometimes it just makes me more frustrated.

When I consider the giants I'm facing—and chances are, you're facing giants too—I need more than simplistic exhortations. I need some real-life, rock-solid reminders that God has not abandoned me. I need some tangible reasons for my hope. That's the wonder of the God Moment Principle. It doesn't just tell me I *ought* to have more faith—it tells me *how*. It's heavenly. It's holy. But it also just makes good, plain sense.

Doesn't it make sense to build your faith on what you *do know* rather than what you *don't know*? There are a lot of things I don't know right now. I don't know why my sister-in-law is standing in line for chemotherapy tomorrow morning at Baptist Hospital rather than for Cinderella's Castle at Disney World. I don't know where Dad might go after his hospital stay. I don't know how we're going to find the emotional energy to parent our two little children, care for our two sick family members, pastor our growing church, and still keep an intimate marriage. I could spend a lot of time focusing on all the things I don't know—and watch my faith erode.

Or I can spend my time rehearsing what I know for sure. For example, I know the very moment in which God called me into the ministry. Just the thought of that holy moment kneeling by the college dormitory couch still brings moisture to my eyes. I look at it this way: If God spoke to me that day sixteen years ago, He'll give me a passionate word to give His people this coming Sunday.

And I know of an even fresher God Moment. My other sister-in-law gave birth to a little boy six weeks ago. The doctors had prepared Anne's pregnant sister for the worst. The fetus isn't growing properly, they told her. The ventricles around the brain are enlarged. The baby will probably suffer a chromosomal defect. At best, surgery after birth. At worst, death. God's people prayed. Six weeks ago we received the phone call. The newborn seems healthy. Medical professionals are scratching their heads in bewilderment. Parents are weeping with joy. We're praising God with renewed faith. After all, here's real fuel for real faith: If God can sustain one sister-in-law, He can sustain the other.

The way in which we remember our lives makes all the difference in how we feel about life today. How much difference? *All* the difference. I think you'll be convinced after hearing another real-life tale.

A TALE OF TWO PARISHIONERS

Two people visited me in my study at different times on the same day. One made me feel good all over. The other made me feel like taking a bath. One visitor was literally the happiest person I knew. The other was the most miserable wretch I'd ever counseled.

Naturally, at the end of the day, my heart paused for some pastoral contemplation about the polar-opposite visits. What caused the stark difference in these two lives? Interestingly, their backgrounds and present-day circumstances were rather similar. Neither had any extra advantages in his or her upbringing. No prestigious family. No luxuries. No college education. No high-paying job. Sadly, both were in difficult marriages and had been disappointed in their children. But despite their similar environments, you'd have thought they had arrived from different planets.

Sandi always sparkled. Always. If you didn't know her, you'd assume that either her smile was phony or her life was trouble free. Some people secretly sneered behind Sandi's back, "I don't know why she puts on that show. Nobody can be happy all the time." Other people quietly mumbled, "Well, if she had the problems I have, she wouldn't seem so happy all the time."

I'll admit that I, too, was suspicious at first. But now I know her well. I was her pastor for nearly eight years. I saw her smile during aggravating committee meetings, and I saw her smile before being wheeled into major surgery. I saw her smile during every sermon and every Bible study. I saw her smile while changing diapers in the nursery and pulling weeds on church work days. Unmistakably, undeniably, her smile was real. Her sparkle was authentic. She was simply a woman of joy.

I knew Sandi had a very difficult husband. In fact, Sandi's husband was profoundly depressed. He attended church but that was about it. He didn't want much to do with Sandi anymore. He wouldn't go out to dinner with her, travel with her, or—many nights—even talk to her. If you've ever lived with someone who acts like they just don't like you, you know it can be a living hell. So I meant it when I asked Sandi, "How are you doing?"

She smiled her prize-winning smile. "I'm doing great. I can't complain about anything."

"Sandi," I responded pastorally, "be honest. Are things the same with your husband? Are you sure you're really hanging in there that well?"

Her smile narrowed enough to let me know that she was going to be totally serious. "Pastor, I really mean it. Sure, things are tough with Sam sometimes, but I love that man. And I believe, one day, God's going to heal him. You just don't know how good the Lord has been to me. When I think about all He's done for me, I can't help but praise Him. I have a wonderful life, Pastor. I don't deserve all the blessings I have. Just pray for Sam—I know the Lord's going to touch him. Now, how can I pray for you and *your* family?"

Conversations like that sometimes leave counselors and pastors scratching their heads and thinking about such words as "denial" and "avoidance." But after eight years of knowing Sandi, I knew this wasn't some sophisticated denial of her problems. This woman was full of faith and authentically happy. I floated higher just for having had the chance to talk to her.

But Butch arrived in my office later that day—and tried to drown me in his pit of quicksand. If you met him, he'd try to pull you in as well. He had come to my office only because his wife had threatened him with divorce. At first he was too angry to talk. As I asked some introductory questions, Butch just sat across from me quivering with rage, his eyes gleaming with hate. When he finally spoke, he spat out his words like you would expel spoiled food from your mouth. He recounted all the reasons for his misery. When his list ended, I asked cautiously, "Butch, I'm sure you've had a lot of pain in your life. But can you remember at least one thing for which you feel thankful?"

Butch stewed for about a minute. Then, solemnly and confidently, he replied, "No, I can't."

Gently, I challenged him. "Take another moment and think. Surely, there is at least one blessing you can point to in your life."

Suddenly my counselee erupted with a furious stream of epithets I cannot repeat. "…Well, Mr. Feel Good, Know-It-All Preacher Man! You have no idea how lousy my life is. I hope someday you'll have something bad happen to *you*. Maybe then you'd know what it's like!"

Later, Butch's wife asked him to move out. Angrily, he did. After a period of separation in which he temporarily began acting like a nice guy, the couple decided to have a date. It was premature and a bad idea. Worse, after dinner, she invited him in and let him spend the night. In the morning, Butch interpreted her actions to mean he was welcome back home. But he wasn't, and she let him know it.

Quietly, methodically, Butch stepped out of the house to his truck, dug out wire clippers, snipped the telephone lines, and reentered the house. He threw his wife to the carpet, clutching her throat. By his own admission, he would have strangled her to death that day, but one of his children toddled into the room. Butch momentarily lost his concentration and his wife escaped.

Thankfully, the woman is now happily remarried. But as far as I know, Butch still stalks her, still hates her, and still can't think of a single blessing in his life. Whenever he crosses my path, he curses me with the same well-rehearsed curses. Sandi, on the other hand, has seen her husband's depression lift and is enjoying a restoration of her marriage.

Two visitors. Same day. Similar backgrounds. Similar circumstances. What powers had gripped them to make them so diametrically different?

It's a question I not only pondered then, but have consistently contemplated in my pastoral ministry. What makes one person full of faith and joy, ready to move forward toward a more abundant life? What makes another person become stuck in a mire of doubt and despair, unable to take positive steps forward?

The difference is remembering the God Moments. Sandi and Butch had similar childhood circumstances, but they remember their lives so differently. She remembers the positive. He remembers the negative. Sandi remembers all the events and circumstances in which God has been active in her past. Butch remembers none. Everywhere Sandi looks, she sees God. Everywhere Butch looks, he sees no God. The difference is not the actual events of their lives. The difference is *how they remember* the events—the God Moments of their histories.

I see the principle at work in everyone I counsel. People full of faith and life regularly rehearse their God Moments. They talk like Sandi: "I don't deserve it, but God has been loving me and leading me." Contrarily, people full of despair regularly rehearse all the ways they feel deprived of blessing. They talk like Butch: "I can't think of a single blessing." Those who meditate on what God has done for them move forward with astounding hope. They are full of God Moments. People who interpret their past as void of God stand still with hopelessness and despair.

HOW DO *YOU* REMEMBER YESTERDAY?

Think about it. *How you remember yesterday determines how you will live tomorrow.* If you primarily remember your successes and triumphs, doesn't it make you think that tomorrow might hold success or triumph as well? If you primarily remember your failures and losses, doesn't it make you think tomorrow might hand you another defeat?

We learn and grow best when we build on positive memories. When you learned to walk as a toddler, how did you do it? Did you dwell on the fact that you had never walked before? Did you try, fail, and then rehearse in your mind over and over how badly you bumped your bottom when you fell? Of course not. Instead, when you took your first steps, you fell. But, amazingly, you somehow *remembered* your success. You remembered what it took to keep your balance and walk. And you built upon that positive memory day by day until you were toddling and giggling all over the house. In fact, I'm quite sure you don't even remember what it was like not to be able to walk.

An unemployed businessman waits outside a manager's door for a job interview. He has a choice. He can rehearse in his mind the painful memory of being downsized, reliving that ugly day when his previous boss gave him the bad news. Or he can rehearse the positive memory of the day he was offered the job in the first place. Which kind of memory will give him a better chance of interviewing successfully for the new position?

A collegiate basketball star stands at the free throw line with two seconds left and an opportunity to win the game. What will help him most in this crucial moment: rehearsing all the shots he has missed, or rehearsing all the ones he's made?

It's clear: There is incredible power in positive memories! If rehearsing positive memories makes a difference for a beginning toddler, a new-hire candidate, or a basketball star with the game on the line, imagine the difference it can make in a Christian's faith.

THE SECRET STRENGTH OF GIANT SLAYERS

King Saul couldn't believe his ears when the pretty-boy son of Jesse volunteered to fight the giant Philistine. Whether the king laughed or cried when he spoke, we'll never know. But the sound of Saul's voice is all too familiar. We've all heard it—the voice that tells us what we can't do. Saul put it plainly to young David: "You are not able to go out against the Philistine and fight him; you are only a boy…" (1 Samuel 17:33).

David could have pondered the monarch's message many ways: A rebuke from the king that allows no response. A welcome opportunity to reconsider a foolishly brave offer. A chance to shrink back and contemplate his youthful immaturity. A moment to rehearse his other failures in life.

But young David's mind raced back to another day. It was a seemingly tranquil pastoral morning. The sheep were feeding contentedly as the musician sat alongside the brook with his harp. Suddenly, birds flapped skyward, sheep scattered wildly, and the shepherd's instrument of praise fell to the ground as David scooped a stone from the stream. A lion leaped from the heart of the Judean wilderness and pounced on a lamb. The boy responded with a heart of courage and attacked the attacker. It was an instinctive, anointed act of bravery.

"Let go of my lamb!" the child warrior must have cried as he hurled the stone that stunned the 350-pound cat. The sheep was freed but the lion was angry. It turned its rage toward the stone thrower. Adrenaline surged. Uncanny strength emerged. Divine energy flowed. David was close enough to grab the matted mane and strike the beast with his staff. The predator slumped into a lifeless pile while the shepherd softly ministered to the wounded lamb.

That's the moment David instinctively remembered while King Saul cursed him with the word "can't." Saul pointed out the boy's limitations, but the anointed shepherd boy pointed to the God Moments of the past:

> "Your servant has been keeping his father's sheep. When a lion or a bear came and carried off a sheep from the flock, I went after it, struck it and rescued the sheep from its mouth. When it turned on me, I seized it by its hair, struck it and killed it. You servant has killed both the lion and the bear; this uncircumcised Philistine will be like one of them, because he has defied the armies of the living God. The Lord who delivered me from the paw of the lion and the paw of the bear will deliver me from the hand of this Philistine." (1 Samuel 17:34–37)

David could have remembered the ways his brothers mocked him. He could have contemplated the humiliation of being sent to the war's front line only to deliver food. He could have looked at the giant and contemplated his own small stature. But David's heart beat with God Moments.

Can you hear the thought process in his mind? *When I did what was right by protecting the sheep, God protected me. It is right to protect Israel, so God will protect me again. Though it seemed foolish to attack a lion, God gave me strength. Though it seems foolish to attack this giant, God will give me strength again.*

A whole army of Israelite soldiers couldn't produce one brave warrior. But one shepherd boy who remembered a God Moment could easily slay a giant.

God Moments will help you face your giants, too.

When the voice of doubt and worry taunts, *You can't fight this battle, you're too———* your best response is the memory of yesterday's victories. When the giants in your path openly mock you with their threats, your greatest line of defense is the recollection of yesterday's predators that have already fallen. Yesterday's God Moments are stones in the sling of faith for tomorrow's giants. How you remember yesterday determines how you will live tomorrow.

YOU'RE MORE THAN A CONQUEROR

Someone will say, "But I didn't kill a bear or a lion yesterday. I haven't won any great battles, slain any life-threatening predators, or seen such miracles."

Oh yes, you have.

Life itself is a battle. There is a constant threat against you. The Scriptures teach that every Christian has a vicious enemy who is a like a lion seeking to devour (1 Peter 5:8). You were given a promise: "You will tread upon the lion...you will trample the great lion" (Psalm 91:13). The fact that you are breathing air, living life, and reading a book is evidence enough that you are a lion slayer. You haven't been devoured yet, have you? You *are* more than a conqueror (Romans 8:37). You may just need to remember your victories.

If David had rehearsed his failures, he surely would have sunk into hopelessness under the sound of Goliath's voice. But the shepherd chose to look for the hand of God at work in his past as the foundation for his faith toward the future. You can make the same choice, and with the same results.

A REVERSAL OF MODERN THERAPY

I, like most pastors and counselors, have spent a lot of time empathizing with parishioners' sad memories because we are called to care for the hurting and weep with those who weep. And I, like most professionals, have spent considerable hours helping people discover hidden, negative memories that have subconsciously haunted them. It's often important that we discover the roots of our pain so the wounds can be truly healed.

But now I realize that for all the hours I have spent helping people recollect their negative memories, I have spent only a fraction of the time helping them discover their positive memories. Most modern therapy, with its Freudian roots, has focused its research and theory on the importance of uncovering painful memories. I agree that repressed pain often needs to surface. But nowhere does God's Word implore believers to devote themselves to finding negative memories. On the contrary: Biblical faith is born from the memory of positive moments of divine intervention.

It literally amounts to a reversal of modern therapy. The key to healing is uncovering positive memories, not negative ones!

If I'm hurting right now (and I am), it's all right to feel the pain and weep the tears. Expression of pain does offer relief, but it doesn't bring hope. How shall I have hope? By choosing to meditate on all the undeniable ways God has blessed me.

The God Moment Principle unveils the answer my heart has so sought. Christian faith is not snatched from thin air. To walk by faith doesn't mean I'm to pull myself up by the bootstraps, pat myself on the back, and tell myself "Everything's just fine." Instead, our faith is built upon the actual, historical activity of God. Faith is rooted in the passionate, redemptive work of God bringing His people from bondage into liberty—first through a sea, then through a cross.

The walk of faith is grounded in a simple conclusion: "If God has brought me thus far, I can trust He'll carry me on."

It's rooted in an eternal promise: "He who began a good work in you will carry it on to completion until the day of Christ Jesus" (Philippians 1:6).

He who delivered me from the mouth of the lion and the paw of the bear will help me kill the next giant as well.

My wife's sister, precious Mary, is hurting so badly today that she can't tie her own shoes. My dad is so incoherent that he's been restrained in his hospital bed. Two infirmities. Two modern-day giants on my battle line. What are yours? I can't offer you a pie-in-the-sky promise about the details of your tomorrow. David didn't know exactly how his battle would unfold. He took five stones but, as it turned out, he needed only one.

I can't predict the details of how God will sustain my family during the difficult days ahead. But I have seen how He has marvelously sustained my life unto this day. Yesterday's limp lions and bears compel me to believe in the tumbling of today's giants. I can't spell out all the ingredients of your future either. But of this I'm confident: If you will join me for this journey into the hidden triumphs of your past life, you will discover enough slain lions and bears to prove God's presence and strength in your life.

As your God Moments grow bigger and stronger, your giants will grow smaller and weaker.

....

CHAPTER TWO

SPIRITUAL AMNESIA

A middle-aged man wakes up next to a rotting mound of trash in a remote part of town and discovers dried blood on his clothes and face. He stumbles toward a rusty, abandoned car and stares at his distorted reflection in the cracked driver's-side mirror. He is looking at himself, but he is looking at a stranger.

The man in the cracked mirror looks totally unfamiliar. Frantically, the bruised, bloodstained man searches his pockets. He has no wallet. No identification. No clue about his own identity.

What would you do if, suddenly, you couldn't remember who you were, where you lived, or if you had a family?

The victim wandered the streets all day, searching faces in the crowds, hoping someone would recognize him. But it was a big city and people hardly looked at him. He spent the night on the street like a homeless person. *Was I a homeless person? Did I have a job?* He couldn't remember any home, but it didn't feel right to be on the street.

The next few nights he spent in a downtown rescue mission. They told him he could stay, but that he would need to find a job. So he cleaned himself up and applied for a job in the biggest building downtown—Lansdowne Corporation.

"What's your name, sir?" the lady asked.

"Er—I'm not sure. Call me Jim, I guess."

"You don't know your name? What's your Social Security number?"

"I don't know that either, ma'am. You see, I was mugged. Everything, including my memory, was stolen. I don't remember anything. I can't even tell you if I have any real job experience. I mean, I'm sure I do. I think I used to do something, I just don't know what."

Jim rambled on pitifully until the lady felt sorry for him. "It's highly irregular," she said. "I don't even know how we can set up our computer for you to get your checks, but I believe you're telling the truth. You can start work tomorrow on the loading dock. You'll be unloading parcel shipments."

Jim worked hard and made enough money to move out of the rescue mission to a run-down, one-room apartment. At night he would toss and turn, trying to remember who he was. The loneliness was overwhelming.

One night he fell asleep long enough to have an odd dream. He saw a woman's smiling face. She was the most beautiful lady Jim had ever seen. He felt himself wanting to run toward her. In coming weeks, the dream would continue and even intensify. But always, as soon as he would try to run toward the beautiful woman, the image would vanish.

After seven months of hard work on the loading dock of the Lansdowne Corporation, Jim was called into the supervisor's office. "Jim, you're one of our best workers. I thought it was risky to hire you in the first place. But because of your hard work and ingenuity, I want to offer you a lower management position. Congratulations. We're proud of your accomplishments."

When the supervisor spoke those words, Jim experienced another flashback. He remembered shaking someone else's hand and hearing those same words. *Congratulations. We're proud of your accomplishments.*

Not many weeks later, Jim left his basement office to run an errand on the ground level of the skyscraper. Then he headed through the revolving doors toward the street for lunch. He was stunned when he saw her. *It's her,* he thought. *My dream lady.* He couldn't stop himself. "Excuse me, ma'am. You look familiar. Uh—are you married?"

The woman looked at Jim's unruly beard and wrinkled shirt. Suddenly she began to weep. "I don't think that's any of your business, sir. Good day." She rushed away. But as she stepped onto the elevator, she turned to look at Jim again.

She was the woman of his dreams, Jim was convinced. What staggered him most was not just the familiar face of the woman, but the feeling he had toward her. He wanted to run to her. He wanted to hold her. He didn't know her name or anything about her, but he *loved* her.

So Jim forgot his lunch and waited for her to leave the building. He caught a taxi and followed her BMW to an exquisite neighborhood. The taxi let Jim out at the corner across from the home of the beautiful lady.

He sat there, gazing, for hours.

Slowly, little flashbacks began leaping through his mind. When a child ran across the front yard laughing, Jim remembered an image of three children jumping around a backyard grill, impatiently waiting for their marshmallows to be roasted. A dog scampered around the driveway with an old shoe in its mouth, and Jim spontaneously said to himself, "He finally got my shoes." The more Jim stared at the house, the faster the images rushed through his mind.

Confused but convinced, Jim rang the front doorbell. When she came to the door, she just stared. Jim broke the silence, "Excuse me, ma'am. I suppose you realize I'm the man who spoke to you at the Lansdowne building earlier. I know this sounds crazy, but please hear me out. A year and a half ago, I woke up in a remote part of town badly beaten and robbed. I couldn't remember who I was or how I got there. Since then I have had no memories except for one recurring dream of a beautiful lady I wanted to hold. When I saw you today, I realized you are the lady in my dreams. And, as I've been watching the house for the last several hours, other images have been returning to me. I remember children laughing around a fiery grill roasting marshmallows. And I remember that old dog stealing my shoes. Does any of this mean anything to you?"

The lady's knees trembled, her lip quivered, and she looked deeply into Jim's face. Tears welled up in her eyes as she exclaimed, "Zach, it's *you!* It's really you. When I saw you today, I thought—but it couldn't be true. We assumed you were dead. But it's you, isn't it? It *is* truly you! Oh, thank God. It's you, Zach. This *is* your home. I'm your wife, Cindy. Do you not remember it all now?"

"I don't remember everything," Zach stuttered. "But I remember I love you and—oh, how I want to hold you. May I?"

She nodded. And as Zach picked her up in his arms, spinning her around, she laughed out loud: "It must be you—you always used to whirl me like that. Oh, Zach, whirl me again!"

He did.

"Don't we have children? Where are they?"

"Zachary, Jenny, Marilyn, Jonathon—come quickly!" Cindy shouted.

As the children pranced into the foyer, one by one, Zach's memory kept returning. "I remember you, I remember you, I remember you, I remember you. Oh, I remember!" He shouted for joy. Then he grew quiet. "But one question. Who am I? What's my last name?"

The youngest child, Jonathon, spoke first. "Dad, we're the Lansdowne family. Your name is Zachary Lansdowne III."

Zach looked at Cindy. "Lansdowne? Like the big building downtown?"

"Of course, darling. You don't know? Your grandfather started the company. You began work there as a teenager in the mail room. After you finished your MBA, he turned the company over to you. You're the CEO and majority stockholder. You moved the business into the new headquarters just a few years ago. All the news stations were there to see the governor shake your hand and tell you how proud he was of all your accomplishments."

After another long embrace, Cindy wiped her tears again and asked the unavoidable question. "Darling, how have you been earning a living for a year and a half?"

"You're never going to believe it." Zach smiled. Then he laughed. "You're just not going to believe it. I never knew a man would lose so much if he lost his memory. If you can't remember your treasures, it's like you don't even have them. Sit down, Cindy—I don't know whether you'll laugh or cry when I tell you the whole story."

I wrote this parable to make a point: The person who loses his memory also loses his blessings. Zachary had a whole, beautiful life; he just wasn't living it. He was blessed beyond measure; he simply had forgotten it all.

I've never known someone with mental amnesia, but I've known a lot of people with spiritual amnesia. It's as though some thief has conked them on the head and stolen their ability to remember anything God has done for them. No matter how greatly God has blessed them, they have totally forgotten it. As a result, they dwell in pessimistic subsistence when they could be living richly in the joy of His blessings.

THE PEOPLE WHO FORGOT GOD'S POWER

You don't have to look far in your Bible to find a bad case of spiritual amnesia. The story of the Exodus shapes the whole memory of Israel. It's a miraculous, moving narrative about a people in bondage who wanted, more than anything, to be free. The book of Exodus tells about the Israelites' release from evil oppression and their escape through impossible circumstances.

You know the story. God raised up Moses, sent him to Pharaoh, and gave him the words to speak. The Lord let forth His glory and wrath upon the Egyptians through a series of unbelievable plagues. Finally, convinced that the Hebrew people were indeed blessed by their God, the heartless Pharaoh consented to let the Israelites go. However, soon after, he changed his mind and unleashed horses and chariots to pursue the escaped slaves.

What ensued was a picture of God's greatness. An impassable sea fronted the Israelites. An invincible army pursued them. The hundreds of thousands of Hebrews were utterly trapped. No way out. Unless...unless they received a miracle.

And then came an awesome God Moment.

God spoke to Moses. The leader raised his staff. The waters rolled apart. The Hebrews walked across the Red Sea on dry land. The pursuing Egyptians were engulfed. The Hebrews danced. The Egyptians mourned.

I can understand why the Israelites celebrated and sang with Miriam, "The Lord is my strength and my song; he has become my salvation. He is my God, and I will praise him, my father's God, and I will exalt him" (Exodus 15:2). I can understand why the prophetess led all the women in a tambourine dance. I can understand why the people rejoiced. But it's difficult to understand what happened next.

In only three days—a long weekend—the Israelites were grumbling. "For three days they traveled in the desert without finding water. When they came to Marah, they could not drink its water because it was bitter.... So the people grumbled..." (Exodus 15:22–24).

If God could negotiate a whole ocean, couldn't He provide a spring of water? The people must have had a memory lapse.

But it wasn't momentary.

God provided sweet water. But in the desert, food was scarce. Suddenly the Israelites were not only grumbling against Moses, they were snorting around the camp: "If only we had died by the Lord's hand in Egypt! There we sat around pots of meat and ate all the food we wanted, but you have brought us out into this desert to starve this entire assembly to death" (Exodus 16:3).

That's no memory lapse. That's spiritual amnesia.

A few desert days and a few missed meals and, suddenly, the memory of the God Moment vanished. It was their choice. In order to make sense of their hungry stomachs and desert circumstances, the grumbling Israelites managed to forget the incredible miracle of their deliverance.

You might be saying, "Well, if God had ever done something so dramatic for me, I'd never forget it. How could somebody forget an incredible miracle like that?" I know how you feel. I used to think that way, too. But now I know that if the Israelites could forget God Moments, so can we. In fact, I see it all the time. Cy Moffitt, a gifted teacher in our church, shared this true, particularly poignant example.

Years ago, Cy was part of a home Bible study group. One of the couples in the group wanted a child; for years they had asked the group to pray for them to conceive. One evening, the couple announced to the Bible study that they had started plans to adopt.

When the couple shared their prayer request, Cy felt the Lord speaking to him. *Ask them if they want their own biological child.* Cy was dumbfounded. What kind of crazy question was that? But the thought wouldn't leave him.

"But Lord," Cy said in his heart, "we've been praying for this couple for years. Of course they want a child of their own. It will be humiliating if I ask them."

Ask them, came the persistent inner voice.

Finally, hesitantly, Cy spoke first to the man: "Do you want to have your own biological child?"

The husband stuttered and finally responded, "Well, of course we do, Cy."

Then Cy turned to the woman. "I think the Lord is asking: Do you want a child of your own?"

The woman, baffled—perhaps perturbed—mumbled something about how long they had prayed for a child.

Cy continued, "Yes, but do you want to conceive a child of your own?"

"Well, yes!" the wife finally answered.

With the whole study group as witnesses, Cy then took a deep breath and boldly shared what the Lord had impressed upon him: that this couple would have a child within the next twelve months. He also expressed his distinct impression that the child would have lots of reddish hair.

The result is easily documented: Eleven months and ten days later, the couple gave birth to their own biological child—a baby boy with "lots of reddish hair."

Give you chills? It should. What a God Moment! What an awesome, loving God we serve! The God who is sovereign over Red Seas is the same God who is sovereign over red-haired boys. Who could forget it?

Well, we could. If the miracle gave you chills, this will give you tears. Cy added, as an afterthought to his story, "Today, that couple is divorced."

I didn't ask about details of the divorce or how it wounded the miracle boy with lots of red hair. But I know this. Somewhere along the line, the couple drifted into a desert. They became hungry. They became bitter. And they forgot how God had sanctioned their marriage and blessed the fruit of their life together. For them to decide that it was better for the red-haired boy to have divorced parents, they had to forget what God had done.

Desert droughts dry up the recollections of dry ocean floors. Momentary adversity distorts memories of joyful moments. Present pain clouds the remembrance of former bliss.

THE MAKING OF A LASTING MEMORY

The Exodus narrative describes the making of spiritual amnesias. At the time of the Red Sea, the Israelites weren't expecting a miracle. They weren't anticipating a God Moment. Instead, they trusted God and celebrated His power only after the miracle's completion. When the days of adversity came, they quickly focused on their lack and let their hearts be filled with fear.

But years later, the people of God would again walk the dry bed of a body of water. Again, the water would be stayed by an unseen power. Again, God's people would march wide-eyed amidst heaped up waves. On this second occasion, too, a leader would be validated and God would be praised. It was another extraordinary God Moment in the life of Israel. Like the Red Sea miracle, the Jordan River crossing was also followed by adversity. In fact, a seemingly impenetrable wall waited at Jericho. But after the crossing of the Jordan, the Israelites didn't buckle in fear and grumbling as they had after the Red Sea. Instead, they recommitted their lives to the Lord and marched on in victory.

Note the differences well, for they reveal how we can prevent spiritual amnesia.

EXPECTANCY

The Jordan crossing was expected. Detailed discussions anticipated the miracle.

> Joshua said to the Israelites, "Come here and listen to the words of the Lord your God. This is how you will know that the living God is among you.... See, the ark of the covenant of the Lord...will go...ahead of you.... As soon as the priests who carry the ark...set foot in the Jordan, its waters flowing downstream will be cut off and stand up in a heap." (Joshua 3:9–13)

Look for God's touch in the midst of your everyday life. Anticipate His move. The more you expect God's hand in your life, the more you will truly notice His work. And the more you will seal the memories of God Moments.

IMMEDIACY

The Jordan God Moment was celebrated as it happened. A memorial was built out of the midst of the miracle.

> So Joshua called together the twelve men...and said to them, "Go over before the ark of the Lord your God into the middle of the Jordan. Each of you is to take up a stone on his shoulder, according to the number of the tribes of the Israelites, to serve as a sign

among you. In the future, when your children ask you, 'What do these stones mean?' tell them that the flow of the Jordan was cut off before the ark.... These stones are to be a memorial to the people of Israel forever." (Joshua 4:4–7)

The Jordan crossing included a deliberate choice to celebrate the miracle *as* it happened, not just *after* it happened. It also included a conscious decision to remember. A pile of rocks served as their memorial to God's faithfulness; that was all it took to seal a memory and teach a future generation. We'll learn a lot more about the power of God Moment memorials later. For now, decide to celebrate your God Moments as they happen and mark them in the midst of the miracle.

THE MEMORY REFRESHER

Here's good news for spiritual amnesiacs: Your memory can return. Here's even better news: God has not left you on your own to remember. Here's the best news: You don't have to know a sophisticated plan. You just need to know a Person.

God has offered you His Spirit to refresh your memory. Before leaving earth, Jesus spent a lot of time with His disciples preparing them for the adversities ahead. He knew they would feel momentarily abandoned. He knew they would be frightened. He knew they would be prone to forget all He had said and done. But instead of prejudging them, He made His beloved an extraordinary promise.

The Lord couldn't have said it more plainly: "The Counselor, the Holy Spirit, whom the Father will send in my name, will teach you all things and will remind you of everything I have said to you" (John 14:25–26). The secret to remembering God's goodness is the power of the Holy Spirit. Perhaps the greatest work of the Holy Spirit in you is to remind you of your God Moments. The Spirit of God is the healer of spiritual amnesia.

Have you found yourself dwelling on hopelessness instead of hope? When confronted with life's giants, has your response been fear instead of faith? You may be suffering from spiritual amnesia. The pages to come offer help and hope. But if you're really going to remember God in your life, it's going to take the power of the Spirit of God. You can be confident when you ask God for His Spirit's help, for His own Son promised: "If you then, though you are evil, know how to give good gifts to your children, how much more will your Father in heaven give the Holy Spirit to those who ask him!" (Luke 11:13).

Whatever time you spend on your knees asking God for the help of His Spirit will be more than worth it. Just remember what Zach was missing—until he remembered. What might you be missing? Isn't it possible that you have a whole secret life of blessing just waiting to be uncovered?

It's time for your spiritual amnesia to be healed. As you read on, I believe you're going to discover a reservoir of sweet recollections. But first, take one important step: *Admit that you are forgetful.* Don't skip this part. You may need to spend substantial time here. It's the essence of real repentance. It's the key to opening your heart to remembering the God Moments of your life. You might pray something like this:

> O God, I'm too forgetful. You have been there for me in countless ways, yet I remember so few. You have parted my troubling seas and I've grumbled in the desert. Help me remember and reclaim the blessings I've forgotten.

Then, ask God for His Spirit to help you:

> Lord, I can't do this on my own. I need a Teacher. I need a Counselor. I need a Helper. I believe Your Spirit can help me, just as Jesus promised. Let the Holy Spirit touch my mind and ignite my heart. Through Jesus Christ, Amen.

....

CHAPTER THREE

"IF ONLY I COULD REMEMBER IT ALL"

"I will meditate on all your works."
(PSALM 77:12)

"Praise the Lord, O my soul, and forget not all his benefits."
(PSALM 103:2)

The word from Psalm 77:12 gripped me. "All." At first, I deemed it just a figure of speech. Like a preacher's exaggeration to make a point. Surely the psalmist didn't mean *all*, literally.

If you're like me, you've meditated upon *some* of God's works—but *all?* I haven't come close to remembering everything God has done for me. The psalmist declares the same message in the Psalm 103 exhortation to "forget not all his benefits." It's another way of saying, "Don't forget *anything* the Lord has done." As I've reread the two psalms, I've become convinced that they mean what they say—*all*. In fact, I believe the psalmist's decision to meditate upon it "all" is the antidote to despair, the ticket to real hope.

Imagine how great the blessing would grow if we *could* remember it all! Think about it. The power of your God Moments grows with each new discovery of God in your past. It's this simple: If remembering a few God Moments strengthens you a little bit, then remembering a lot of God Moments will strengthen you a lot.

Here's how it works. You might be forgetful, but you haven't forgotten every good thing. You can recount a few memorable moments that have made you feel valuable or loved or strong. From time to time, those God Moment memories dance in your mind. And when your mind dances with those joyful thoughts, your heart usually joins your mind on the dance floor. When your heart starts dancing with joy, your whole being feels like dancing too. Isn't it amazing? Just a few powerful memories—and next thing you know, you're having a ball!

The problem, for most people, isn't remembering *something*. The problem is remembering *many things*. Your memories of God Moments are wonderful, but they're just too scarce. So those few positive memories only make it to the dance floor occasionally. When the memories dance, it's great while it lasts. But then the dance floor gets crowded with busyness or anxiety, and suddenly, the music stops. Homecoming is over and it's a long time until the prom.

So don't seek to remember only the obvious, magnificent God Moments. Let your heart meditate upon *all* the incredible, intricate ways in which God has been at work blessing you throughout your life.

Perhaps an earthly example will help you get started.

Late one Saturday night while trying to tidy up my sermon, I lost myself in thoughts of the next day. Mother's Day. I started thinking of all the things Mom did for me that I had never thanked her for—things I'd never even considered. I grabbed a pen and began writing Mom a note. Her blessings in my life weren't difficult to remember once I started. But the list was hard to finish.

Dear Mom,

If only I could remember all you've done for me, I could say thank you.

I wish I could remember what it was like for you when I was waiting to be born. It was cozy for me during those nine months. I just floated and relaxed. What was it like for you? I hope you weren't prone to morning sickness. Were you? And did you get tired often? I've watched my wife during her first trimester—she salivates at the mere sight of a couch. You had two little boys in one small house back then. Let's see, while I was on the way, Mark was one, David was two. How did you find time to be tired with two toddlers? I wish I could remember so I could say thank you.

What was your labor like? Did you have to work until

exhaustion set in? Or did you have to put up with the side effects of anesthesia? I wish I could remember so I could say thank you for bringing me into the world.

How did you make room for me in the little house on Pershing Court? Did you just let me sleep in your room? Did I cry much at night? How much sleep did you get that first year of my life? Dad was doing the late weather then, wasn't he? Did you wait up for him to get home, even though you had toddlers waking up early the next morning and me crying in the night? I wish I could remember so I could say thank you.

If I hadn't come along, the Pershing Court house would probably have been big enough, wouldn't it? That first year of my life, you built a new house on Pinetop Road. You made it big enough for me to have my own room. I bet it was a stretch financially. I wonder what you went without in order to make space for me. I wish I could remember so I could say thank you.

How did you have time to hold me and cuddle me that first year? I figure you must have hugged me a lot, because I hug Bennett a lot. I wish I could remember what it felt like, as a baby, to fall asleep in your arms so I could say thank you for rocking me.

How did you keep an ear out for me when I took naps? You didn't have baby monitors in those days. I guess you had to stay close by. I wish I could remember so I could say thank you.

Did you use cloth diapers or disposable? It seems I remember you mentioning cloth. Yikes! Did you have a diaper service? I hope so. How many diapers of mine did you change? Did I spit up much? Did I (I hate to ask) spit up on you? I'm glad I forgot, but I wish I could remember if I threw up on you so I could say thank you for not throwing me out.

How did I learn to walk? Were you cheering me on, picking me up whenever I fell? Were my older brothers prone to wallop me without thinking? How did you protect me that first year? I wish I could remember so I could say thank you for guarding my life.

When I was two and you let Bob come over to play, it was

more trouble to have one more kid to watch, wasn't it? Did you have to solve disputes over toys, wipe tears, and prepare snacks for my playmate? I wish I could remember so I could say thank you.

What did you do for my two-year birthday party? I bet you baked a cake. Did you ice it and decorate it yourself? I wish I could remember so I could say thank you.

When did I start getting all those earaches? How many trips did you make to Dr. Benbow with me? When did I get my adenoids taken out? How did you manage to be with me in the hospital and still take care of my brothers? Hey, what year was it that I drank the dog's water and got dysentery? And when did I fall back in my high chair at the kitchen table and cut my chin wide open? How many stitches was that? How many times did you fill the vaporizer and "Vicks" me so I could breathe better when I had a cold? I wish I could remember so I could say thank you.

What was the name of that lady at the playschool who didn't smell so good? I can still remember her smell, but I can't remember how many times you carpooled me over there or how many of my drawings you put on the refrigerator. I wish I could remember so I could say thank you.

What about all those pets? When did we have the cats? When did we get our first dog? What actually happened to Lucky? Did anybody ever feed Brownie but you? I wish I could remember so I could say thank you.

How many tennis tournaments, soccer matches, hockey games, and football games did you watch me play? I looked for you in the stands every time. I just never counted how many games. I wish I could remember so I could say thank you.

And when things got so painful in your marriage, how many nights did you cry after I went to bed? What does a single mom do? Is that when you learned to cry out to God? How many times did you take me over to Armand and Nancy's so they could pray for me? I wish I could remember so I could say thank you.

And how many secret hours did you intercede for me? When I was so shy and scared, how did you convince me that I was special and loved? How did you coerce me to recount my blessings every night even though I thought it uncool? I wish I could remember so I could say thank you.

What about my teenage years? What made you keep wanting to be around me when I acted like I didn't want to be around you? And, Mom, what did you do at home alone all those nights that I was over at my girlfriend's house, looking for a family in her family? And when I was in college and didn't write or call very much, how did you keep writing and calling me? I wish I could remember so I could say thank you.

And, Mom, when you kept my little boy recently, did you take a walk and feed the ducks? Did you rock him too? Did you sing to him too? Did you pray for him too? If only I knew, I could say thank you.

Mom, my memory's not very good about all these things because I was too busy living my little life to notice much. But I'm starting to remember. It happens little by little. Like last night when I changed my boy's wet sheets or this afternoon when I wanted to take a nap but had a toddler on my ankles. I'm starting to remember. Bear with me, it's not going to all come back at once. But I choose to meditate upon your love because it makes me feel all the more loved. And as my memory of you grows, so does my gratitude. And, Mom, though my memory may fail, my love for you never will. Have a happy, unforgettable, Mother's Day.

Love,
Alan

I'm sure Mom thought my note was a gift to her. But I assure you, the note was a gift to me. The Mom Moments I remember are a true blessing to my heart. As more and more memories surface, I am even further blessed.

Now imagine the blessing of remembering *God* Moments.

And imagine what it would be like if you could remember *everything* God has done for you.

Imagine witnessing His hands knitting you together in your mother's womb.

What if you could recall the sight of God's cosmic paintbrush dabbing you with that freckle or filling in the color of your eyes?

How would it make you feel if you could remember Him gently tugging on each of your hairs as He was numbering them?

Imagine seeing the quantity and description of the angels God assigned to you at birth.

Imagine remembering all the times your life was in danger…but one of your angels brandished his sword and fought back your enemy.

Imagine watching the pen of eternity in the hand of the Author as it inscribed your name in the Book of Life.

Imagine peering into the heavenlies and hearing the voice of God announcing to the cherubim all the plans He had for you.

It might move you to a prayer such as this one:

Lord, I wish I could remember all You have done for me—so I could say thank You. Be patient with me, Lord. My memory isn't very good. I've been too busy and concerned about my own life to notice Your life in me. But it's coming back to me little by little. Bear with me—and help me through Your Holy Spirit. I choose to meditate upon *all* Your works and consider all Your mighty deeds. Not just a few, isolated deeds. All of them. Because the more I remember of You, the more I feel loved. The more I am loved, the more I can love. As my memory grows, so does my gratitude. As my gratitude grows, so does my desire to love You with my whole heart. Thank You, Lord—for everything.

Love,
Your Child

....

CHAPTER FOUR

THE FIVE KINDS OF GOD MOMENTS

*A*t the beach recently, I chuckled as I watched two would-be treasure hunters at work. They weren't sailing to an ancient shipwreck for a deep-sea diving expedition. They weren't following a long-lost treasure map to find a hidden grotto containing old pirate treasures. But in their own way, they were treasure hunters. They were combing the beach with metal detectors.

It must have been a man and wife—looked to be in their sixties. Little Bennett and I were playing on the beach in our shorts. They had on the traditional metal-detector garb—long johns (well, I'm just guessing), old sweat suit, loose-fitting windbreaker with hood (always up, of course), and a plastic bag for treasures. Dragging a shovel in one hand, wearing headphones for the thrilling beeps, the metal-detector people walked back and forth, methodically sweeping the disk above the sand. Just walking, listening, and occasionally digging up a lost dime or old beer bottle cap.

The scene is amusing to me because, first, I'm sure they find more beer bottle caps than old dimes. Amusing, also, because I'm sure they will never, in a lifetime, find enough old dimes to cover the cost of their metal detector. Amusing, finally, because even if they hit the mother lode and find a lost silver dollar or a corroded wristwatch, it would still take a week to find enough money or watches to match what they could have made at a real job in an hour.

THE GOD MOMENT PRINCIPLE

But I don't chuckle at the metal-detector couple for long—I come from the same breed of animal. You do, too. Isn't there something great about getting something you didn't have to produce? Isn't there a certain exhilaration when you unearth a hidden treasure? There's a special sense of reward when you happen upon something that was previously hidden.

Part of the thrill of God Moments is that you don't produce them—you just unearth them.

But, like beachcombing treasure hunters, you need to look in the right places and you need to look methodically. Notice that the metal-detecting couple wasn't hovering over asphalt streets which could not be dug or where nothing was lost. They weren't sweeping the dunes where no one ever walked. They were looking where "treasures" were likely to be found. They looked methodically, not randomly.

The moments of God's intervention and blessing in your life and mine are unspeakably vast—beautifully varied. Just telling you to search for God Moments in your past would be like telling the metal-detector man to search the whole world. It would be overwhelming.

A random search will not produce near the results of an organized search. It's best to look for God Moments in your past by searching the places His hand is most likely to be found. As a result of studying the feasts of Israel, the stories of Scripture, the testimony of hundreds of parishioners, and the experience of my own life, I believe God's blessings tend to fall into five kinds of God Moments. Those five categories will serve as our treasure map.

THE GOD MOMENT FEASTS

Believe it or not, Leviticus 23 is one of the most important chapters in the whole Old Testament. It describes the feasts of Israel, around which the whole life of Israel revolved. The appointed feasts of the Lord were the primary tool of memory for the Hebrew people. The whole reason God prescribed the feasts was so that His people would not forget His power and blessing. The feasts were, simply put, the commemoration of God Moments. In coming chapters, we're going to see how those ancient, Hebrew festivals offer life-giving principles for our modern-day faith.

There were seven feasts commanded by the Lord that occurred during three seasons in the Hebrew year. Like the seven-candle menorah, the Hebrew feasts were grouped as three, one, three (three feasts in the spring, one in the summer, three in the fall). The three spring festivals were celebrated in close proximity as were the three fall festivals. So every year, Hebrew pilgrims would travel to Jerusalem three times—spring, summer, and fall—for a week or more each time.

A quick look at the feasts of Israel can help us realize and appreciate the timeless nature of five very special kinds of God Moments in our lives.

THE GOD MOMENT OF AMAZING RESCUES

The Destroyer moved through Egypt killing every firstborn child—except in the Hebrew homes. The blood they placed on their doorposts was a sign: God would not allow the Destroyer in. The Feast of the Passover serves as a reminder that God rescued His people then—and now:

- An inexperienced teenage driver can't make a turn. The car rolls several times. It was a convertible with the top down. The teenager walks away unharmed. How?
- A mother carrying an infant in his portable car seat tumbles down two flights of steps, dropping the seat as she falls. The baby slides down the steps in his bouncy seat like a sled on a snowy hill. Neither is hurt. Why not?
- A tornado rips through a nearby neighborhood. A ride by the devastation would convince you that no one survived. The paper reports no casualties. How could it be?

THE GOD MOMENT OF HOLY ATTRACTION

In the Feast of Unleavened Bread, no Hebrew home is allowed to have any leaven or yeast in the house for seven days. Yeast represents sin. There must be none. When the house is cleansed, the children search for the last crumb of leavened bread. Once found, the father (not the children) removes it. God was at work purifying His people then—and now:

- A teenage girl nervously enters her boyfriend's bedroom. His parents are out of town. She feels strangely repulsed by what she is about to do. Suddenly she pushes herself away, saying, "No, I don't want to do this." What force made her desire purity?

- A businessman sits at his desk preparing a memo that would cover his mistake with a distortion of truth. Suddenly, he hits the delete key and starts over: *The truth is…* What makes a man decide to be honest in a world full of lies?
- A thief loses sleep and finally calls the police. What makes a robber turn himself in?

THE GOD MOMENT OF UNEARNED BLESSING

During the Feast of First Fruits, the people offer the first of their harvest to God. You can't make something grow by yourself. Planting a seed is an act of faith, but God is the One who gives the growth. God gave His people what they couldn't give themselves because the Lord provided surprise blessings then—and now:

- A husband calls his wife with delight in his voice: "Honey, I got a promotion!" "How wonderful," she responds. "What for?" The man scratches his head. "I'm not sure." What causes a man to receive a surprise reward?
- A farmer wipes the sweat from his brow, looks at the best soybean crop he's ever had. The weather has been perfect. What causes a good season?
- A lonely, elderly man sits on a bench. A young woman sits beside him and tells him a sweet story that makes the man laugh—and makes his day. Who sent the young woman into his life?

THE GOD MOMENT OF REVEALED TRUTH

God's people gathered at Sinai to hear the word of the Lord. Amidst the wind and fire, God spoke. Fifteen hundred years later, New Testament believers gathered in Jerusalem, waiting for the Spirit. Each heard the gospel in his own language because God was speaking to all. The Lord revealed truth then—and now:

- A husband and wife are celebrating their tenth anniversary when the woman asks her beloved, "How did you know I was the one?" The husband smiles and says simply, "I just knew." How did he "just know"?
- During the Sunday message, a parishioner quietly weeps in her

pew. *How did the preacher know what I was going through?* How did he?

- A businessman retires after forty years in a job he loved. He thinks to himself: *Coming to work here was the best decision I ever made. I hate to think what would have happened if I had taken that other job.* Was it a "good decision" or had he been spoken to?

THE GOD MOMENT OF VALUABLE ADVERSITY

Even the wealthiest mansion-dwelling Hebrew was required, for a week, to live in a hut in the desert just as his forefathers had. The Festival of Booths is a tangible reminder that God, not houses made with hands, is our dwelling place. It is a reminder that even though they were in the desert, God sustained His people. God was preparing them for the Promised Land. God is so powerful that He could turn desert days into something good then—and now:

- A middle-aged couple watch their home movies and laugh. The husband remarks, "Those were the hardest years of our lives, weren't they?" The wife responds, "Yes. And the best." How can hard years be such good years?
- A man gazes out the window of his new office and rejoices silently, *This is the job I always wanted. And just think, if I hadn't been downsized from the other company, I would have never made this step.* Sometimes the low moments give birth to the best moments, don't they?
- After being dumped by her live-in boyfriend, a single woman weeps in her bedroom. In her pain, she calls out to God for the first time: "God, are you there? I need you...." Pain can bring a person to her knees.

GOD MOMENT	FEAST	SEASON	COMMEMORATION	SPIRITUAL BENEFIT
Amazing Rescue: *You were guarded or set free*	Passover	Spring	Last plague; escape from slavery; "Passed Over"	Peace
Holy Attraction: *You were cleansed or drawn to something noble*	Unleavened Bread	Spring	Remove yeast or leaven—symbolizes removing sin	Obedience
Unearned Blessing: *You were given a blessing you couldn't have attained for yourself*	First Fruits	Spring	First harvest of the year; Thanksgiving for blessing	Joy
Revealed Truth: *God spoke to you or led you*	Feast of Weeks	Late Spring	According to tradition, giving of law at Sinai	Confidence
Revealed Truth	Feast of Trumpets	Early Fall	Blowing shofar; call to gather	Confidence
Holy Attraction	Day of Atonement (Yom Kippur)	Fall	High Priest into Holy of Holies; sacrifice for sins	Obedience
Valuable Adversity: *God sustained you during a difficult time and prepared you for a greater blessing*	Feast of Booths	Fall	Lived in huts while wandering in wilderness on way to Promised Land; God our dwelling place	Perseverance

oday, as Christians, we are not bound by Jewish law. Instead, we live by a greater law—the law of freedom in the Holy Spirit. We're not required to follow festival details three times a year. Instead, God calls us to Spirit-led living 365 days a year.

Like the feasts, though, the God Moment Principle is much more than a stroll down memory lane; it's a reenactment of God's intervention in our lives. It's more than a pleasant return to bygone years; it's an absolutely essential practice for real-life faith.

Now let the treasure hunt begin. I think I hear your metal detector beeping. But be assured, as we look into the loving ways of God we will find no old dimes or rusty beer bottle caps. No cheap metal trinkets. Instead, we're going to unearth treasure beyond measure as we remember—and draw strength from—the God Moments of our lives.

....

CHAPTER FIVE

AMAZING RESCUE

The First Kind of God Moment

*P*astor, do you mind if I bring the coat to show them?"
"Keith," I responded, "if I were you, I'd not only show it, I'd have it framed and hanging on my bedroom wall. By all means, bring the coat—and the bullet, too."

Keith told our congregation about his God Moment. He showed the coat. He showed the bullet. But mostly, he showed God's work of Amazing Rescue. Listen as Keith tells it:

It was about 10 P.M. I needed to pick up some cash for my golf game the next day, so I drove to the bank ATM that I frequently used. I don't know why—I didn't usually do it—but that night, something told me to leave the car's engine running and the door open. As I pulled my cash from the machine, I noticed several men across the parking lot. I turned back toward my car. That's when I saw them sprinting toward me. I knew it was bad. I jumped into the car. As I was throwing the gear shift into drive, I looked up and they were on me. The leader had a pistol pointed at me. The threat to my life was only inches away.

Instinctively, I stepped on the gas. As I did, I saw the blast from the pistol. I remember the explosion as the bullet passed through the glass. I remember what the smoke looked like as it rolled out from the gun. I remember feeling the hot impact of the bullet in my right side. As I screeched away, I pressed the wound tightly to try to prevent blood loss.

I chose to pull into my neighbor's driveway. He's a doctor and I knew he would be able to take any lifesaving measures necessary. I would be safe there until the ambulance arrived. Stunned and weak, I made my way to his door.

"I've been shot!"

My neighbor quickly took me inside. Carefully, he positioned me on my back.

"Where's the wound? Your side? Yes, I see the bullet hole. Okay, let's remove your coat to see the wound."

He removed my leather coat carefully. Then, seeing another bullet hole in my shirt, he removed my shirt as well. Then came the moment neither he nor I nor anyone else could believe.

The bullet fell out from between my shirt and my skin.

"The skin is unbroken," my friend exclaimed. "The bullet didn't penetrate your skin at all. Unbelievable!"

The only wound was a burn mark—the silly result of my tight pressure against the hot, freshly fired bullet against my bare skin! Authorities could hardly believe the account. As an attempt to explain the mystery, the police report recorded the bullet as hitting my belt. But it wasn't even close to my belt. See?

That's when Keith held up the coat for the congregation.

He cried. I cried. We all applauded.

Then Keith showed the intact bullet; it still had most of its point. Despite the police report, and despite others' speculation, no one can explain why Keith didn't suffer major injury or die that night. No one, that is, except Keith. He knows what happened.

It was a God Moment.

It was a moment that built Keith's faith in a God who protects. It proved to him that (I can't resist saying it) God's grace is faster than a speeding bullet.

We don't live by the measure of our experiences. We live by the measure of God's Word. But one good experience of the reality of God's Word will make the Scriptures explode within you. Imagine the verses that must have leaped to Keith's mind:

> "Are you not much more valuable than [the sparrows]? Who of you by worrying can add a single hour to his life?" (Matthew 6:26–27);
> "It is not by sword or spear that the Lord saves; for the battle is the Lord's" (1 Samuel 17:47);
> "'Not by might nor by power, but by my Spirit,' says the Lord" (Zechariah 4:6);
> "Do not be afraid, for I am with you" (Isaiah 43:5).

It's remarkable. God used a moment of intense fear to bring Keith lasting peace. Others have survived traumatic events only to let the moment of danger make them more worried about future crises. But Keith's experience brings him lasting peace because he remembers it as a God Moment.

*O*n May 1995, Randy Reed, a thirty-four-year-old construction worker, was welding atop a nearly completed water tower outside Chicago. According to one writer, Reed unhooked his safety gear to reach for some pipes. A metal cage slipped and bumped the scaffolding on which Reed was standing. The scaffolding tipped. Reed slipped.

He fell 110 feet facedown in a pile of dirt. He barely missed the rocks and construction debris. When paramedics arrived, Reed was breathing. When they hoisted him onto the backboard and began carrying him to the ambulance, Reed spoke. The man who had fallen 110 feet and lived had enough energy to speak. You're not going to believe what he said.

"Don't drop me."[3]

By the way, doctors said that Reed came away from the accident with only a bruised lung. His three words were probably an attempt at humor from a miracle man with a really bad backache. But what a picture of the human tendency. A man who lives through a 110-foot plummet is worried about a possible three-foot fall.

God knew the Israelites would tremble in the face of big opponents, so He gave them a tool for confidence:

> You may say to yourselves, "These nations are stronger than we are. How can we drive them out?" But do not be afraid of them; remember well what the Lord your God did to Pharaoh and to all Egypt. You saw with your own eyes the great trials, the miraculous signs and wonders, the mighty hand and outstretched arm, with which the Lord your God brought you out. (Deuteronomy 7:17–19)

But the Israelites, like us, tended to do just the opposite of the mandate. Instead of facing threats with the powerful God Moments of yesterday in mind, they usually focused on the size of their foes. The spies that explored the Promised Land typify the human heart that concentrates on the obstacles in the future rather than the faithfulness of God in the past.

> But the men who had gone up with him said, "We can't attack those people; they are stronger than we are." And they spread among the Israelites a bad report about the land they had explored. They said, "The land we explored devours those living in it. All the people we saw there are of great size.... We seemed like grasshoppers in our own eyes, and we looked the same to them." (Numbers 13:31–33)

A preacher once had a bad flight. One bumpy flight and for the rest of his life he hated airplanes. One time he sat down next to a calm passenger who noticed the preacher's nerves. "Why are you afraid, Preacher?" the passenger asked. "Doesn't that Bible of yours say that God is with you always?"

"No, that's not exactly what the Bible says," the minister responded. "The Bible says, 'Lo, I am with you always.'"

Why do we remember the few air-travel tragedies instead of marveling in memory of the thousands of planes that land safely every day?

Why do we remember the minuscule number of children who have been abducted from playgrounds instead of remembering the millions who have frolicked in parks unbothered?

Why do we remember the handful of swimmers bitten by sharks instead of the zillions of summer vacationers who have splashed in the waves all day long?

God knew the sinful heart's propensity to fall into fear. Only fear, not the enemy armies, could keep the Israelites from the Promised Land. The answer to fear is remembering well what the Lord has done to yesterday's enemies. Like the children of Israel, we must train our minds so that when we face a great obstacle, we immediately remember God's faithfulness in the past.

HOW REMEMBERING AMAZING RESCUES BRINGS PEACE

At the heart of the Ten Commandments stands the mandate: "Observe the Sabbath.... On it you shall not do any work." It's the command to rest—to quit striving—to be at peace. We all know it as God's law. But have you ever noticed the Deuteronomic prescription for observing the Sabbath? Read it closely: "Remember that you were slaves in Egypt and that the Lord your God brought you out of there with a mighty hand and an outstretched arm. Therefore the Lord your God has commanded you to observe the Sabbath day" (Deuteronomy 5:15). If you can't remember God's protection in the past, you'll have a hard time truly relaxing today. Remembering God's rescue yesterday is the key to being able to rest today. Knowing your God Moments brings true peace.

The Passover is the key God Moment of Amazing Rescue. We get the word "Passover" from the Hebrews' adaptation of an Egyptian word *pesak*. The Hebrew root connotes a mother hen covering her little ones with her wings. The English rendering gives us the sense of God "passing over" the Hebrew homes where there was blood on the doorposts. But review the story carefully. God did more than "pass over" the Hebrew homes. He *rescued* the Hebrew homes.

"When the Lord goes through the land to strike down the Egyptians, he will see the blood on the top and sides of the doorframe and will pass over that doorway, and he will not permit the destroyer to enter your houses and strike you down" (Exodus 12:23). *He will not permit the Destroyer to enter.* God was actively protecting His people. God wasn't merely *omitting* His people from calamity—He was *rescuing* them from certain death. The Passover feast commemorates this Amazing Rescue when God blocked the Destroyer from consuming His people.

I am thoroughly convinced that God is actively blocking the Destroyer from consuming you and me—day by day, moment by moment. Our world is not a safe place. High-speed cars. Unpredictable weather patterns. Deadly microscopic viruses. Contaminated foods. Unexpected events. Inexplicable hate crimes. Nuclear warheads. Need I continue? The world is an ominous place in which to live. We are ants trying to make it across a Manhattan sidewalk. Which brings us to some serious questions:

How have any of us made it safely thus far?

Why haven't we all been hit by lightning or swept away in a tornado?

Why haven't we all broken our necks or been hit by a drunk driver?

God is a rescuer, moment by moment.

Of course, we're not going to simply forget former traumas as though they never happened. In fact, we need to remember yesterday's bitter threats in order to appreciate the sweetness of salvation. The Passover (or *Seder*) meal includes dipping a leafy green vegetable into salt water or vinegar so each participant will taste its bitterness. It shows on their faces: a picture of the bitterness of slavery, the bitter bite of bondage. Later in the meal, participants eat a sandwichlike mixture of two pieces of unleavened bread (*matzo*) with a sweet apple spread in the center. The sweet sandwich is dipped into horseradish sauce. It's a bittersweet bite. The Hebrews needed to remember the terrible threat of oppression in order to

GOD MOMENT MEMO

PASSOVER

When? The first spring feast, March–April.

What? Symbolic meal of lamb, bitter herbs, and unleavened bread.

Why? To remember how the Lord protected and delivered Israel by protecting Hebrew homes.

Scriptures: Exodus 12:1–14; Leviticus 23:5; Numbers 28:16–25; John 2:13; Hebrews 11:28.

The God Moment: Amazing Rescue.

The Spiritual Benefit: Peace.

remember the joy of real liberation. They needed to remember the ominous Destroyer that engulfed Egypt in order to remember the wonder of being rescued. Likewise, we must remember how dangerous life is in order to remember how greatly God has been at work saving us.

UNCOVERING YOUR GOD MOMENTS OF AMAZING RESCUE

When I first discovered the power of remembering God Moments, my little boy was three years old. It happened one ordinary Thursday night after Anne, Bennett, and I met some other family members for dinner at a favorite restaurant. A quick review of the evening made me realize that I had been constantly at work saving Bennett's life—and he didn't even know it! In one evening I had:

- pulled the boy back into his high chair just as he was making it tip backward—saving him a trip to the emergency room;
- pulled the boy away from his ice cream bowl when I recognized that he was about to eat five adult portions himself—saving him from a gigantic bellyache;
- pulled the large, steel steak knife away from him after he grabbed it from someone else's place setting—sparing him a gaping flesh wound;
- pulled him close enough to silence his excited screams—saving us all from flesh wounds from the other restaurant patrons;
- pulled the boy back as he darted straight into the parking lot where there were moving cars;
- insisted that he sit in his designated car seat with the seat belt attached;
- once home, assured that his bathwater was not scorching hot and that he did not intentionally swallow so much toothpaste as to bring on the bellyache I'd rescued him from in the restaurant;
- gave him only one vitamin when he wanted the whole jar;
- knelt by his bed and prayed, "Oh God, keep your angels over my boy."

In the course of one ordinary evening, I rescued my boy dozens of times. If a sinful, earthly father is that hard at work protecting his little boy, how much more is the perfect heavenly Father at work rescuing His little ones?

You may never have faced a plague like the last one that hit Egypt, and you may have never had a bullet stop without piercing your skin, but the truth is that God has been at work rescuing you every day. We don't have a God who once wound up the world and now simply lets it run like a clock. Instead, He governs every tick, every breath, every moment. He numbers every hair on every head. He knows every thought in every mind. He hears every prayer in every heart.

So let your God Moment treasure hunt start here: Consider how dangerous the world is. This is not an invitation to dwell upon the few moments in which you experienced great pain or loss. Instead, take this opportunity to meditate on the amazing circumstances that have enabled you to live as long and as well as you have. Start with your earliest memories. Think back through your life carefully. Pay special attention to pivotal moments of danger from which you escaped.

GOD MOMENT MEMO

UNCOVERING YOUR GOD MOMENTS
OF AMAZING RESCUE

1. Acknowledge how dangerous life is.
2. Begin with childhood memories—it seems we're especially protected by angels then.
3. Recall the pivotal moments of near-accidents, major mishaps, or life-threatening circumstances which you have survived.
4. Pay special attention to illnesses from which you have recovered. All healing is actually a rescue from danger and is ultimately from God.
5. Acknowledge moments of foolishness that could have brought you harm but didn't.

THE WAYS GOD RESCUES PEOPLE

After I spoke in church about the God Moment of Amazing Rescue, one parishioner remembered a moment many years earlier that he had assumed was simply good fortune.

As Noel Reubel was driving one day, he noticed a group of rough-looking guys slowly cruising behind an older woman as she walked alone. Noel decided to offer the lady a ride home. After delivering her safely, Noel was waiting at a stoplight when he noticed the same rough-looking guys in the car next to him. They got out of their car; so did Noel. Then he saw their chains and other weapons and realized he was in deep trouble.

Suddenly, seemingly from nowhere, a car pulled up behind them. Out stepped a man who, in Noel's words, "was one of the most imposing men" he had ever seen. His mere presence proved to be lifesaving. Few words were spoken, but the suddenly timid men jumped back in their car and drove away. As Noel returned to his car, he looked back at the big man to thank him…but his rescuer was gone. Noel had never seen the man before and he never saw him again. For nearly twenty years after that day, Noel assumed he had enjoyed a stroke of good luck. Now, after understanding God Moments, he says, "God sent that man. He must have been an angel!"

My wife was recently carrying our newborn down the steps in the baby-bouncy seat. Anne said it felt like something literally reached up and tripped her. She fell headlong down two flights, dropping the baby in the fall. At the bottom of the steps my helpless wife looked up to see tiny Abigail's bouncy seat stay upright—and slide down the steps like a tobog-gan on a snowy hill. Mom and baby were startled but totally unharmed.

Once my brother, David, pulled into a McDonald's parking lot with his young son. Something in his heart felt uneasy, whispering, *Wait*. So David and his son waited a moment in the car. They heard a *bang*. It could have been an exploding tire, but David pulled out of the parking lot immediately. He later saw it on the news: armed robbery and a shooting at McDonald's. But it was more than that to my brother. It was a God Moment.

In his senior year of high school, my other brother, Mark, was in a horrible van accident. The van flipped numerous times. Mark was unhurt. His friend, the driver, was hospitalized but eventually recovered.

The accident was a painful moment, but it was a God Moment.

Last year a rare tornado ripped through our city. One drive past the devastation would make you think hundreds had been killed, but no one was. It was a tragic moment. It meant homelessness for dozens of people, including a good friend of ours. But for the survivors, it was a God Moment.

Preacher, radio host, and author Duane Miller spent months of his life with no voice. Something had killed the nerve endings that controlled his vocal cords. It was an incurable and untreatable condition. He had lost everything—his vocation, his preaching, his confidence. His only ministry was teaching a Sunday school class at First Baptist Church in Houston. With a specially designed microphone and amplification, Duane could squeak words in a raspy whisper. One Sunday morning, he began teaching on Psalm 103:2: "Praise the Lord, O my soul, and forget not all his benefits—who forgives all your sins and heals all your diseases, who redeems your life from the pit...."

When Duane spoke the words "redeems your life from the pit," a miracle happened. His voice suddenly came back. It's the most medically verifiable miracle I've ever known. In fact, the miracle was recorded on audiotape. Now, every day, every moment, Duane Miller remembers the God Moment in which God rescued his voice.

GOD HAS RESCUED YOU FOR A PURPOSE

It was July 1, 1945. The war was over. A young soldier named Stanley decided to take a few friends and go visit his brother, Charlie, in Darmstadt, Germany. Bill, Bruce, and Herb made the trip with Stanley. They spent the day with Charlie, did a little shopping, and, at day's end, drove the Autobahn along the Rhine River back toward Stuttgart. The sky was growing dark. Bill was driving too fast. The potholes that had been created by months of mortar blasts had yet to be repaired.

Driving over a knoll, with no indication of a coming crater, Bill had to swerve suddenly. The front tire hit the curb and the vehicle tumbled, over and over. Finally it came to a stop, upside down. Stanley slid himself out of the jeep.

"Bill, Bruce, Herb! Are you guys okay?" The question was met with silence. Stanley was the only one conscious. The others were badly injured.

He hailed a truck. "Help! Wounded here!"

As the men from the truck were unloading blankets, Stanley momentarily forgot his friends. He reached out his hand for a blanket with a muttered, "Thank you."

"No!" a man hollered. "These blankets are for the wounded."

Stanley remembers it this way: "For months, I had looked down on the other men because they weren't 'fine Christians' like me. I had considered them drinkers and carousers. But instantly, my pharisaical feeling of moral superiority vanished. There I was, unhurt, and my three friends were dying. I was broken by the discovery of my own selfishness."

Back at the Stuttgart hospital, Stanley visited his unconscious friends. As he sat in the waiting room, he overheard doctors using vulgarities and even cursing at the unconscious patients. Inside his heart, Stanley told himself, *Maybe someday I'll be in a position to help people, and I'll never treat men like this.*

As Stanley prayed for his unconscious friends, he also considered the weight of his own sin. Instead of asking, "Why did this tragedy happen to them?" he began asking, "Why did I escape the tragedy?" Instead of "Why them?" he asked "Why me?"

Stanley Bennett is my wife's uncle—and a mentor to me. He has also been an evangelist to the lost, a pastor to a flock, a missionary to Brazil, a counselor to hundreds. I have heard that story, or parts of it, at most family gatherings. How could he not share it? For this was the moment Stanley realized God had rescued him for a purpose. It was the birth of his calling into ministry.

God has rescued you for a reason, too. He has a destiny for your life. It might not be to preach in a Brazilian jungle. It might never bring you fame. But you were not saved by chance and you do not live by chance.

$\mathcal{A}$ woman made a foolish turn in her automobile and hit another car. Nervously, she wiped tears from her eyes and opened the glove compartment in search of her registration and insurance card. As she fumbled around, a note fell out. It was her husband's writing. Imagine the calm that came when she read the words: *Honey, in case of an accident, remember: It's you I love, not the car.*

Whatever a person loves most is what he most wants to protect.

So how much must God love you?

Our childhood dog was a brown mixed mutt of minimal intelligence, but we loved him. Though a small, relatively weak dog, Brownie was strangely courageous if one of us was nearby. On one occasion, Blackie, the biggest, strongest, meanest dog in the neighborhood, growled at Brownie. Brownie foolishly growled back. The terrible fight that ensued could not be broken by a full-force water hose or even a board broken over Blackie's back. Blackie was poised to strike the death bite to poor Brownie's neck when, suddenly, my brother Mark did an incredible thing. A remarkable, stupid thing. He dove into the dog fight. As Mark grabbed Brownie, Blackie clamped his teeth on Mark's shoulder instead of Brownie's neck.

Brownie went home and ate some dog food, drank some water, and took a nap. Mark went to the hospital for stitches and shots. It made no sense, did it? A boy taking the bite for a dog....

You know what else doesn't make sense? A shepherd jumping in to protect a sheep from a lion. "I am the good shepherd," Jesus said. "The good shepherd lays down his life for the sheep" (John 10:11). A shepherd taking the bite for a sheep. Why?

Because a person rescues what he loves. Two thousand years ago, a Nazarene was nailed to a cross and, in that moment, the Messiah rescued you from the pit of death. It was an Amazing Rescue.

Ever since, over and over, God has rescued you in ways you may have hardly noticed.

Why?

A person rescues what he loves.

....

CHAPTER SIX

HOLY
ATTRACTION

The Second Kind of God Moment

he Feast of Unleavened Bread required the Hebrew people to engage in the original "spring cleaning." Every Hebrew family would literally scrub the house down to make sure there were no undetected crumbs of leavened bread. The law commanded it: "Remove the yeast from your houses, for whoever eats anything with yeast in it…must be cut off from Israel" (Exodus 12:15).

The yeast is symbolic. When the Israelites left the land of their slavery, there was no time to wait for bread to rise. When God delivers His people from bondage, He wants nothing to delay their freedom. Yeast, which puffs up bread, is a picture of sin, which puffs up the human heart. A little leaven affects the whole loaf. A little corruption affects the whole body. A little sin can detain you from entering the Promised Land. That's why Paul told the Corinthians, "Get rid of the old yeast that you may be a new batch without yeast—as you really are" (1 Corinthians 5:7).

Though the cleanup festival required active participation from the whole family, a fascinating tradition emerged in Jewish homes during the Feast of Unleavened Bread. After the home had been thoroughly cleaned—floors scrubbed, pots scalded, and sheets boiled—the Hebrew father would hide a tiny piece of leavened bread. The children were then let loose for a hunt. When a child found the yeasted bread crumb, he dared not touch it. Instead, the boy or girl called Daddy, who would arrive with a feather and a wooden spoon. With the gentleness of a feather, the father brushed the crumb onto the wooden spoon, carried it outside, and threw it into a fire.

How many times in your life have you unsuccessfully tried to hide your sin? You might expect the heavenly Father to bring a steel hammer to crush it out of you or a fire hose to blast it out of you. Indeed, the eternal hater of all sin will, in the end, tolerate no wickedness. But haven't you found that the Holy Spirit most often comes not with a blasting hammer or a blistering hose, but with a feather? There is an incredible wideness and patience to the mercy of God. There is an astonishing gentleness to the work of God in making us more holy.

Consider the picture of the Hebrew father, and him alone, having the authority to feather-brush the final crumb. The children recognize the leavened crumb, but the daddy removes it. The festival paints a vivid, prophetic picture: Father God is the only One who can make us holy. The Feast of Unleavened Bread is prophetically fulfilled in Jesus Christ, the Bread of Life, who was utterly "unleavened"—completely without sin. The way to purity is through *His* cleansing work, not our own works of righteousness, that anyone should boast. Even the conviction of sin, the remorse we feel over our wrongdoing, is the work of the Holy Spirit (John 16:8).

The Holy Spirit convicts you. So it is God Himself who plants the desire in your heart for a cleaner life.

Christ, by His shed blood, washes you. So it is God Himself who makes you clean. One of the most beautiful and prevalent ways God has been at work in your life is by feather-brushing away the corruption that would keep you in the land of your bondage. Every moment in which you have felt convicted of selfishness and drawn toward a holier way is a God Moment. They are the God Moments of Holy Attraction. Remembering the moments of Holy Attraction in your past will foster a joyful obedience to God's will.

MY MOMENT OF HOLY ATTRACTION

As happens to so many Christian college students, my freshman year of undergraduate school brought intellectual conflict crashing against the evangelical faith of my teenage years. My mind and heart wrestled one another until my soul became restless and worried. By my junior year,

GOD MOMENTS MEMO

THE FESTIVAL OF UNLEAVENED BREAD
When? The second of the spring feasts.
What? Clearing the home of yeast; eating only unleavened bread.
Why? To remember that God is at work cleansing our lives from sin.
Scriptures: Exodus 12:15–20; 13:3–10; 23:15; 34:18; Leviticus 23:6–8; see also 1 Corinthians 5:7.
The God Moment: Holy Attraction.
The Spiritual Benefit: Renewed Obedience.

though I had probably demonstrated the appearance of Christian contentment, there was a full-fledged war at work within me that often kept me up at nights. Little did I realize that I was actually warring against God's will for my life. And how little did I understand God's great ability to win any war He wants to win!

Even then, I loved God's Word. I wanted to learn about God and teach others about Him—but I didn't want to be a minister. Of course I didn't want to be a minister. Who does? I had always been "one of the guys." I wanted to stay "one of the guys." I didn't want to be isolated into some ministerial pigeonhole that would exclude me from normalcy. I wanted to teach God's Word, but I didn't want to be called "preacher." So I decided to become a professor. It's a wonderful profession. A life of teaching can be one of life's great callings. And, I thought, if I were a professor, who wouldn't be proud of me? It seemed the perfect path for me to satisfy all my desires. (Did you hear that? A path for *me*. *My* desires.)

That is, until the God Moment.

One night in the fall of 1983, I knelt to pray next to the little red couch in my third-floor room at Stacy dormitory at the University of North Carolina at Chapel Hill. That little couch, which had stood in the corner of my childhood room on Pinetop Road and would one day be tossed from the third-floor window of Stacy dorm, was, that night, my holy altar. Inexplicably, I was drawn to pray fervently. Though I had seldom knelt for prayer previously, that night I did. Though I often prayed silently, that night I prayed out loud.

Though my memory fogs about the names of my professors, about friends in my dorm, and even about entire courses I took for credit, the details of that holy moment are locked away in my mind and heart forever. I remember the Presence like one remembers an aroma from an enchanted hideaway. With briefly closed eyes and a simple, spontaneous recollection, I can feel the blanketlike warmth of the Presence the way a bride remembers her groom's wedding-night embrace. With even brief meditation upon the holy encounter, my heart still beats wildly, my mouth grows mute, and my eyes dampen again. I'll simply never forget it. Never.

Like all profound spiritual experiences, words fall embarrassingly short of the real encounter. And, also like all personal encounters with God, some of it is simply too intimate to share. Let me begin by clarifying something: *It just happened.* I'd like to say I did something especially faithful to make it happen, but I didn't. Though I prayed fervently that evening, I was no giant of prayer. Though I was seeking God, I can't say I was panting after Him like the deer after the waterbrook. I just knelt and prayed, and God chose to come near.

I had thought about holiness, even studied the subject. But that night I experienced the mystery. Like Rudolph Otto's classic description of holy encounters, I experienced a tremendous awe that might make a man cover his face and run. At the same time, I felt a mysterious fascination with the Holy Presence. For a few life-changing moments, God let me see the weight of my sin. For a few life-changing moments, God let me feel the weight of His glory.

I was overcome by this compelling, holy love that had come into my dorm room like an encompassing cloud. Instantly I saw the selfishness of my soul. I had charted my course without any real consultation with my Maker. I was, at the same time, utterly undone over my sin and intensely drawn toward this beautiful, pure Presence that had begun filling my heart.

I wept openly, profusely, passionately. I cried tears that I didn't know I had. It was as though some deep well of repentance suddenly became an artesian spring. But in the midst of the emotional flood there came the most intense peace I had ever known. I suddenly wanted what the Holy Presence wanted. I felt my soul being washed. And, in the midst of the moment, God spoke distinctly to my heart. It was so simple. So beautifully, quietly simple.

Alan, you know I've called you into the ministry, don't you?

"Yes, Lord, I know. Oh, how I want to follow You."

That was it. A moment that changed my entire destiny. I told my roommates that evening. I called my mom that night. And, never—not once—in my ensuing sixteen years of study and ministry, have I questioned, doubted, or forgotten that moment. A moment that would shape every detail of my life and would move me down the narrow path God had ordained for me. A path of unspeakable blessing. I absolutely love being a minister of Jesus Christ.

The most fascinating facet of that holy encounter was not hearing God call me into the ministry—though I remain awed that He wanted me to serve Him. I am not most overwhelmed by my recollection of the great gush of emotion—though the well of tears still surfaces at times. Rather, in contemplation of that call experience, one fact astonishes me more than all the other facets combined:

I was suddenly attracted toward that which had previously repelled me.

I was left with two questions that have only one possible answer: Why would I be drawn passionately toward selflessness when I had been living such an openly self-seeking life? Why would I be intensely attracted to surrender the life I had so carefully been clinging to?

The answer: I had experienced a God Moment of Holy Attraction.

You certainly don't have to be a preacher to experience it. You, too, have had moments of Holy Attraction. Everyone has.

Every Christian is a Christian only because a holy God made Himself attractive. Jesus said it plainly: "No one can come to me unless the Father who sent me draws him" (John 6:44). Every person who has yet to commit to Christ has likewise been attracted by His holiness. "For since the creation of the world God's invisible qualities—his eternal power and divine nature—have been clearly seen, being understood from what has been made, so that men are without excuse" (Romans 1:20). Every time you have avoided the trap of sin…every incidence in which you opted for high moral standards…every decision for purity…every lovely thought…is a God Moment of Holy Attraction.

Human beings are born in sin and, apart from God, live with sin-tainted spectacles that color every aspect of life. We are not naturally drawn toward God—we are *supernaturally* drawn toward Him. The human heart is utterly alienated from God. James boldly states that our friendship with the world is hatred toward God (James 4:4). Have you done some rotten things in your life? If so, I'm not surprised. You were born in sin just as I was. Have you done some wonderfully pure things in your life? Now that surprises me! I can't explain why you would aspire toward something noble or holy—but for the God Moment of Holy Attraction.

WHY YOU DIDN'T EAT PIG SLOP FOR BREAKFAST

"There was a man who had two sons. The younger one said to his father, 'Father, give me my share of the estate.' So he divided his property between them" (Luke 15:11).

The opening sentence of Jesus' famous parable is staggering. Kenneth Bailey describes the stabbing pain the father must have felt upon hearing the son's request:

> For over fifteen years I have been asking people of all walks of life, from Morocco to India and from Turkey to Sudan, about the implications of a son's request for his inheritance while the father is still living. The answer has always been emphatically the same…. The conversation runs as follows:
> "Has anyone ever made such a request in your village?"
> "Never!"
> "Could anyone ever make such a request?"
> "Impossible."
> "If anyone ever did, what would happen?"
> "His father would beat him, of course!"
> "Why?"
> "The request means that he wants his father dead."[4]

Bailey explains that, normally, after signing over his possessions to his son, the father still is entitled to live off the proceeds. Because the younger son of Jesus' parable demands and gets the full use of the inheritance before the father's death, the implication is agonizing. It is as though the boy said, "Father, I would rather you were dead."

Pause at those words. *"Father, I would rather you were dead."* Put yourself in the place of the father long enough to feel the piercing of his heart. Once you begin to feel the deep sting, consider God's own heart. Every child of God who seeks his own way rather than God's way, every disciple who denies Him, every self-centered life, has virtually communicated the same message to God: *"Father, I would rather you were dead."*

I would have expected the father to simply decline. I would not be surprised if the father had beaten the boy into submission, shamed him into staying, or physically restrained him from leaving. But what the text next tells us so matter-of-factly begs belief: "So he [the father] divided his property between them."

The father could have kept his son home by fear or by force. He could have made a dozen plans by which to sabotage the boy's folly. Once the boy was gone, the wealthy patriarch could have sent servants to recapture the carousing kid. But from the beginning, the father decided to rely on a different strategy. He would let the boy become repulsed with his own folly and be drawn back to the father who had always loved him.

It was risky but simple. The father, by loving his boy anyway, would allow the beauty and blessing of home to travel in the son's wayward heart until, eventually, it would draw him home.

The younger son tried to live it up and wound up barely living at all. One day, destitute, hungry, and working in pig pens, he actually considered eating the pigs' slop. He had reached the depths of his waywardness—not because he thought of eating food fit for pigs, but because pigs were unclean to the Hebrew people. He was not only associating with the defiled creatures—he had become like swine.

The marvel of the God Moment of Holy Attraction is not that God has always prevented you from taking an ugly path, but that in the depths of your ugliness God has still called you homeward. To discover moments of Holy Attraction, you'll need to take a painful look at the moments in which you resisted God's way the most. Take an honest look at your life and identify the painful moments in which you, in one way or another, said, "Father, I would rather you were dead."

The younger son reached total emptiness—of belly and of heart—before he came to his senses and said, "How many of my father's hired men have food to spare, and here I am starving to death! I will set out and go back to my father" (Luke 15:17–18). Please don't miss this. The boy came home because he was attracted to his father. The boy came home because he was inwardly drawn to his father's blessing. Stop and ponder the unspeakable power of a father's lifelong blessing hidden in a wayward son's heart. The attraction of home was so compelling that it overcame the boy's shame, folly, and stubbornness. It was, of course, the boy's choice to return, yet it was an irresistible attraction.

Amid the snorting of the hogs, the boy somehow heard the sound of childhood laughter in his own backyard. In plain view of the pig waste, he somehow saw his father's smile. While still breathing in the crude odor of swine swill in a faraway land, the foolish son somehow smelled lamb chops sizzling on his father's grill.

The only way the foolish son ever found his way home was by the stunning attraction of a better, holier, healthier way. It was a moment of Holy Attraction. It's the only way anyone finds the heavenly Father's feast.

UNCOVERING YOUR MOMENTS OF HOLY ATTRACTION

Any moment in which you, like the younger son, "came to your senses" was a moment of Holy Attraction. You might have said, "I recognized the error of my ways" or "I just couldn't rest," but you took the path to purity only because God was at work in your life.

Holy Attraction means discovering the sweetness of God's way compared to your own way:

> The commands of the Lord are radiant,
>   giving light to the eyes.
> The fear of the Lord is pure,
>   enduring forever.
> The ordinances of the Lord are sure
>   and altogether righteous.
> They are more precious than gold,

> than much pure gold;
> they are sweeter than honey,
> than honey from the comb. (Psalm 19:8–10)

Holy Attraction means that God is the one doing the purifying work, not us: "After he had provided purification for sins, he sat down at the right hand of the Majesty in heaven" (Hebrews 1:3).

In unearthing the treasure of Holy Attraction moments, begin by thanking God for sending His only Son for you while you were still in sin. Ponder the initiative of God in your salvation. Praise Him for loving you while you were still in a faraway land.

Next, reconsider the low moments in your moral life. Look closely at the times in which you were attracted to unhealthy things. What has made you less interested in things that can destroy you? Before you just pat yourself on the back for "kicking the habit" or putting away a sin by sheer willpower, ask yourself: *Why did I feel compelled to change?* Don't gloss over the times of youthful foolishness. What has made you want to mature in your character, your relationships, your walk with God? If you've lived a relatively pure life, praise God for the factors that have made you want to steer clear of ungodliness. What people or influences has God put in your life that showed you the benefits of purity?

Finally, don't presume that your own effort to clean up your life has ever been sufficient. Instead of taking credit for your cleanliness, learn to pray as David did for deeper attraction to holiness:

> Cleanse me with hyssop, and I will be clean;
> wash me, and I will be whiter than snow....
> Hide your face from my sins
> and blot out all my iniquity.
> Create in me a pure heart, O God,
> and renew a steadfast spirit within me. (Psalm 51:7–10)

HOW REMEMBERING HOLY ATTRACTION MOMENTS RENEWS OBEDIENCE

Last week my little boy took a bad tumble. I had warned him repeatedly about walking on the brick retaining wall that sides our driveway. But he figured he knew better. My wife heard his screams and raced to the front

GOD MOMENTS MEMO

FINDING MOMENTS OF HOLY ATTRACTION

1. Remember your faraway lands. Reexamine the times your morality, purity, and obedience was low in comparison to where you are now. Acknowledge God's attractiveness.
2. Replay moments in your mind when you opted for purity. If there are big moments—turning down an invitation to adultery, refusing an opportunity for dishonest riches— remember those first. But consider all the smaller ways God has been drawing you toward holiness:
   - choosing a good set of friends;
   - wanting to give money to a charity;
   - telling a cashier she gave you too much change;
   - turning off an ugly movie;
   - reading a book like this one.
3. Ponder the means by which God has attracted you to His ways:
   - What people have made you hungry for holiness?
   - What events have opened your eyes to God's goodness?
   - What inner longings have emerged in your heart that steered you toward purity?

door to see the hysterical boy pitifully attempting to walk up the sidewalk to the house. Thankfully, he had sustained only a flesh wound to his leg— no emergency room trip this time. When I joined them in the kitchen for an inspection of the injury, it took tremendous parental restraint to fight back frustrated words of disappointment in him. Thankfully, I restrained an angry "I told you so" and managed to add some comfort as I assessed the wound.

Bennett must have cried for twenty minutes straight. It was a bad scrape, and it looked like it really hurt. Finally, our tearful son blurted out: "Now I know why you don't want me walking on that wall!"

My heart melted. It hadn't required my shameful reproach, or, in this case, even my discipline to teach Bennett. Instead, the pain of his folly suddenly was undesirable to him and he was attracted to my commandment. I don't think I'll have to caution him about that wall again.

We can be obedient by sheer willpower for a little while. But eventually, temptation overcomes us and we fall off our walls as well. There, as we wallow in pig slop or weep over a bleeding leg, God is at work wooing us. Something within us knows there is a better way. The better way becomes strangely attractive. That attraction toward holiness has an infinitely greater power to keep us obedient to God's Word than our own willpower.

I don't go through a week, possibly even a day, without remembering how God called me to the ministry. I recognize how big a mistake I would have made had God not attracted me to His will. I recognize how much more blessed I am having been irresistibly drawn to His plan. The memory of that special moment in which I was attracted to His holiness makes me want to follow Him all the more.

Rehearsing the God Moments of Holy Attraction will refresh your heart with the confidence that God's way is the best way. Every time you remember being attracted toward a more holy or noble path, you will also recall that God's way is the way to abundant life. Remembering that lamb chops are better than pig slop is remembering that the Father's table is always richer. The more you remember the way the path of purity has blessed you, the more eager you are to obey the Father. Remembering moments of Holy Attraction produces willing, grateful obedience in your heart.

Are you walking in the will of God? Wonderful. Remember the God Moments that have brought you to your current discipleship. Keep the memories fresh. They will keep you hungering for purity. Have you turned away from the heavenly Father? Are you in a faraway land? If so, ponder deeply the times you took God's way rather than your own. Hasn't God's way always been better? Turn your nose away from the swine slop. Lift your head heavenward and breathe in the delectable smell of lamb chops on the Father's grill. Look heavenward and see the smile on Daddy's face. Listen heavenward and hear the laughter in the yard.

The memories of Holy Attraction are calling again.

Come home.

....

UNEARNED
BLESSING

The Third Kind of God Moment

've never seen anyone dance like A. C. Never mind the fact that this saint is in his late seventies. He moves with a sophisticated step but a simple heart. Gliding with precision, he keeps an air of whimsy about him. Sure, he taught dance at the Arthur Murray studio years ago, but it's not his training that makes his dance beautiful. A. C.'s dance is like his heart—light, grateful, expectant.

It's amazing how differently a man lives if a dance lives in his heart. As I came to know the man, I became more interested in this dancing spirit's genesis than I was in the dance itself. Where did A. C.'s levity of heart and love for life begin?

Let me tell you how I learned about the God Moment that made A. C. Williams's heart dance.

I was still new to my first pastorate in Durham, North Carolina, but our small congregation had begun growing. In an effort to make more parking available, we had scraped together the budget to pour gravel in a cleared field adjacent to our existing, paved parking lot. I was saying good-bye to the last few worshipers after a Sunday morning service when A. C. came back to speak to me.

"I don't want to sound too strange," he said. "But the Lord told me to come back in here and speak to you. That gravel out there is no good. It's going to tear up the ladies' shoes. We need to pave that lot. Get in touch with me and I'll pay to have that parking lot paved."

I smiled politely and thought about this man who seemed of moderate means. *He doesn't know how much asphalt costs.* But, of course, I called him.

As it turned out, he indeed knew how much asphalt costs. And indeed he was ready to pay for it. So A. C. and I got together for lunch.

I didn't start our conversation with the paving project. I started with A. C. Any man who's nearing eighty, still works hard every day, dances lightly every Friday night, and paves parking lots for growing churches is a man I want to know. What makes a positive man tick? What was the source of his joy? What was at the root of his generosity? It took only a simple question to find out: "Tell me about yourself."

Immediately, A. C.'s mind flashed back to his childhood, to a God Moment that had changed his heart sixty years earlier. Hear A. C. tell it.

*M*y family was poor. My father was a tobacco farmer, and we all worked the farm. One day my mother told me it was more blessed to give than to receive, and I laughed at her. 'Ha, you give me a brand-new football and I'll tell you if it feels better to give or receive,' I said. It wasn't until years later that I found out she was right.

"I was fifteen the day I decided to thumb a ride from my home in Middlesex in Nash County to the big city of Durham. My uncle Elmer helped me get a job with the Western Union delivering telegrams for twenty-five cents a day. Every Christmas I'd go home and take Santa Claus to the family off my earnings. When winter passed each year, I'd get a letter saying Daddy needed my help on the farm. So I'd go home for the summer and help. But I would come back to Durham in the fall.

"I got a bed at the Salvation Army and met a boy who told me he had heard I was in town. This boy, whom I'd never met, befriended me and told me, 'If you go to the U-Drive-It place and tell Mr. Johnson you need a job, he'll give you one.' So I went. Sure enough, the next morning I had a job at the U-Drive-It shop.

"Some time later, that same boy dropped by the U-Drive-It. 'I hear they're hiring down at the American Tobacco plant,' he said. 'Those are high-paying jobs.' Well, I knew I'd never get one of those jobs. Why, the people would be lined up all the way down the street. What did I have going for me? But the boy insisted, so I finally gave in and went."

A. C. paused amidst the story and became pensive. "Why did that boy help me? He wasn't even a friend. There wasn't anything in it for him."

He continued the story. "We walked four blocks across town. As I had imagined, we couldn't get close to the door. We just sat down by the railroad tracks on the hill above the crowd of applicants. There were hundreds of people waiting, pressing in toward the door. I was telling the boy with me, 'We don't have any chance of getting ahead of these people,' when a man opened the door.

"'Ya'll can go on home now—we aren't hiring anymore,' he told the crowd.

"As people began leaving, the strangest thing happened. The man paused, looked in my direction, pointed and hollered out: 'Do you want a job?'

"The boy elbowed my side. 'Hey, he's talking to you!'

"'No way in the world,' I said. 'That man doesn't know me—he can't be pointing at me.'

"But, Pastor," A. C.'s voice broke, "he *was* pointing at me. Why? Can you tell me why that man picked me out of that crowd? The next day I went to work at one of the best-paying jobs a boy could ever get—sacking tobacco for six dollars a day. My first paycheck was forty-two dollars. I'd never seen so much money in all my life. Why did that man pick me out?"

"A. C., I think I know and I think you've always known, too," I answered. "God gave you that job, didn't He?"

A. C., now blurry-eyed, nodded his head. Then he added, "You see, I was just a poor boy from Nash County who didn't have a chance in the world until that man picked me out of that great big crowd. It's only gotten better and better for me since then. I never thought I'd have any money, but God has now blessed me so much. I've learned that my mother was right. It *is* more blessed to give than to receive. Now, about that parking lot...."

A. C. paved the lot and the next one, too. He gave the first major chunk of money to start our building fund for a new sanctuary. He's still giving. Still dancing. And he still can't forget the day a man picked him out of the crowd for a job he didn't deserve.

A. C. was transformed by the power of a God Moment. Once you get to know A. C., you'll discover plenty of hardship in his life. You'll hear about some tough times in his early childhood. You'll hear about his beloved wife's long bout, and eventual death, of multiple sclerosis. Sure, A. C. has had hardships. Everyone has. But A. C.'s dance of life is fueled by the constant rehearsal of an Unearned Blessing that came his way more than sixty years ago.

If you recognize and rehearse the fact that God has given you a life-changing gift—a job, a spiritual gift, a friend, a mate, an opportunity, a calling—a dance will be born in your heart, too.

WHY THE KING DANCED

More than a thousand years before Christ, another man danced. He had no Arthur Murray training, and his steps were not nearly as sophisticated as A. C.'s. But his dance was born in the same womb—a God Moment of Unearned Blessing.

The Jebusites were proud of their position in the small, twelve-acre city. The steep city walls atop two canyons made them haughty in the face of young King David's fighting men: "You will not get in here; even the blind and the lame can ward you off" (2 Samuel 5:6). The Jebusites shouldn't have laughed.

David was as undeterred by the holy city's occupants as he had been by the Philistine giant. David took his throne to Jerusalem. Before that, he took the Ark of the Covenant. Before that, he took his dance.

Oh, how he danced.

> So David went down and brought up the ark of God from the house of Obed-Edom to the City of David with rejoicing. When those who were carrying the ark of the Lord had taken six steps, he sacrificed a bull and a fattened calf. David, wearing a linen ephod, danced before the LORD with all his might, while he and the entire house of Israel brought up the ark of the LORD with shouts and the sound of trumpets. (2 Samuel 6:12–15).

David laid down his robe. He laid down his royal raiment. He laid down his pride. The Hebrew text suggests it was a free, whirling dance. Pure celebration, overt gratitude, awesome praise.

The Hebrew peasant girls celebrated, but Israel's First Lady watched with disdain. Michal could not join in the unguarded praise. She spat out words of sarcasm: "How the king of Israel has distinguished himself today."

The prideful queen couldn't possibly understand. She was a king's daughter, raised in royalty, reared with riches. She couldn't fathom what it was like for a forgotten shepherd boy to become king of God's people. But David remembered it all. His response to Michal reveals the God Moment in which his dance was born.

"David said to Michal, 'It was before the LORD, who chose me rather than your father or anyone from his house when he appointed me ruler over the LORD's people Israel—I will celebrate before the LORD'" (2 Samuel 6:21).

Consider the answers the king *might* have blurted back to his haughty wife:

"I have fought battle after battle. I have put my neck on the line time and time again. I have proven myself to be a great warrior and leader. This is my moment in the sun, don't block my rays."

"I put up with your father's pitiful antics long enough. He's dead now. I've won. I don't care how bitter you are about your dad's death. He's gone. I'm here."

"I am a man of many talents. It was my harp that soothed your neurotic dad. It was my sling that slew Goliath. It was my plan that gained me the throne. Out of the way, woman, let me dance."

But listen again to David's actual response: "It was before the LORD, who chose me rather than your father...when he appointed me ruler." God chose. God appointed. God is responsible for this blessing, not me.

David's mind returned to a quiet day he had spent with the sheep in the Bethlehem fields. While the boy shepherd talked to his lambs, his brothers were talking to the prophet of God. David's dad, Jesse, had lined up his older, taller boys for Samuel. After looking at all the likely candidates for the throne, Samuel baffled Jesse with his words: "The LORD has not chosen these.... Are these all the sons you have?"

"There is still the youngest," Jesse answered, "but he is tending the sheep" (1 Samuel 16:10–11).

In the presence of David's brothers, the man of God took the horn of oil and poured it out upon the shepherd boy. Samuel poured the oil; God poured the blessing. David stood still. All he could do was receive the gift—and receive he did. The oil flowed down as freely as the gift of anointing would flow henceforth in the shepherd boy's life. Others watched in awe as the unprovoked love of God showered a youngster with grace. The Bible says simply, "from that day on the Spirit of the LORD came upon David in power" (1 Samuel 16:13).

David never forgot the day of that Unearned Blessing. Others might look at his military prowess, his boyish good looks, his musical talent, or his winsome personality to explain his success. Michal would have preferred her husband boast of his accomplishments than dance with abandon. But David knew the truth. God had plucked him out of the shepherd's fields in Bethlehem to make him shepherd over Israel. So his answer to Michal was spontaneous: "God gave me this. I didn't earn it. I didn't win it. He just chose me. So I must dance in praise."

HOW REMEMBERING UNEARNED BLESSINGS BRINGS REAL JOY

The God Moment of Unearned Blessing is the antidote to foolish pride. It is the secret to lasting joy.

If you celebrate what you feel to be your own accomplishments, your celebration will be temporary. Soon you will anxiously seek another foe to defeat in order to recapture the good feeling. Contrarily, when you celebrate an Unearned Blessing, you celebrate the eternal love of God in which He has chosen you before the foundation of the world (Ephesians 1:4).

There is far greater joy knowing that you have been chosen than knowing you are skillful. If your joy is dependent upon your own skillful accomplishments, it is a fragile, expendable happiness that will evaporate at the first sign of potential defeat. If you find your happiness in what you have earned, you are subject to abject despair when you can no longer grasp prizes by your own prowess. Ultimately the life that celebrates the mere human spirit is paralyzed by fear, for it knows that the human spirit cannot always conquer its heavily armored Goliaths or its steep-walled Jerusalems.

When we forget the God Moments of Unearned Blessings we embrace a primal sin: pride. "Pride goes before destruction, a haughty spirit before a fall" (Proverbs 16:18). Remembering Unearned Blessings is therefore essential for healthy life. The Scriptures show the God Moment mandate to be inextricably linked with the memory of Unearned Blessing:

> When the LORD your God brings you into the land he swore to your fathers, to Abraham, Isaac and Jacob, to give you—a land with large, flourishing cities you did not build, houses filled with all kinds of good things you did not provide, wells you did not dig, and vineyards and olive groves you did not plant—then when you eat and are satisfied, be careful that you do not forget the LORD, who brought you out of Egypt, out of the land of slavery. (Deuteronomy 6:10–12)
>
> When you have eaten and are satisfied, praise the LORD your God for the good land he has given you. Be careful that you do not forget the LORD your God, failing to observe his commands, his laws and his decrees that I am giving you this day. Otherwise, when you eat and are satisfied, when you build fine houses and settle down, and when your herds and flocks grow large and your silver and gold increase and all you have is multiplied, then your heart will become proud and you will forget the LORD your God, who brought you out of Egypt, out of the land of slavery.... You may say to yourself, "My power and the strength of my hands have produced this wealth for me." But remember the LORD your God, for it is he who gives you the ability to produce wealth, and so confirms his covenant, which he swore to your forefathers, as it is today. (Deuteronomy 8:10–18)

THE FEAST OF FIRSTFRUITS

The commanded spring festival of Firstfruits specifically reminded the Israelites that God, and God alone, grants us the greatest blessings of life. The festival occurs in conjunction with the first harvest of the year. "The LORD said to Moses, 'Speak to the Israelites and say to them: "When you enter the land I am going to give you and you reap its harvest, bring to the priest a sheaf of the first grain you harvest. He is to wave the sheaf before the LORD."'" (Leviticus 23:9–11). Note the emphasis again, "the land I am going to *give* you." God gives the land. God gives the sun. God gives the rain. And God gives the growth. Like a tithe, the first tenth of our income, the Firstfruits offering made the people of God remember that the whole coming harvest was God's gift.

The Firstfruits festival was filled with joy. Joy in the thought of being chosen. Joy in the knowledge of living in God's affection. Joy in the promise of a greater harvest in the future. The God Moments of Unearned Blessing are a foretaste of the joy of heaven. Though we acknowledge the inevitability of death, "Christ has indeed been raised from the dead, the firstfruits of those who have fallen asleep" (1 Corinthians 15:20). Though we groan inwardly amidst the travails of life, we have the firstfruits of the Spirit (Romans 8:23) reminding us of the lavish grace of God. Ultimately, the great abiding bliss of the Christian's life is rooted in a God Moment of Unearned Blessing—the joy of our salvation.

UNCOVERING YOUR UNEARNED BLESSINGS

Joy is built on a simple, powerful, reliable cycle ordained by God.

The more my heart dances before God, the less credit I take for the good things that have happened in my life. The less credit I take for the

GOD MOMENTS MEMO

THE FESTIVAL OF FIRSTFRUITS
When? The third of the spring feasts associated with the Feast of Unleavened Bread.
What? Presenting a sheaf of the first of the barley harvest as a wave offering.
Why? To remember that God, not human effort, grants the harvest. To remember God's goodness.
Scriptures: Leviticus 23:9–14. See also Romans 8:23; 1 Corinthians 15:20–23.
The God Moment: Unearned Blessing.
The Spiritual Benefit: Lasting Joy.

good things in my life, the more God Moments of Unearned Blessing I discover. The more God Moments I discover, the more I am filled with joy and praise. The more I praise God, the less credit I take for the good things that have happened in my life.

Of course, there is happiness in accomplishment. And there's nothing wrong with taking pleasure in a job well done. Personal achievements can bring satisfying feelings of self-respect, self-confidence, and self-worth. It's nice to feel good about yourself and what you have earned. But it's nothing compared to the unspeakable joy of apprehended grace.

The joy of Unearned Blessings is built upon an incredible awareness: *If it's not all up to me, then anything can happen.* To acknowledge your inability to manufacture your own blessings is to open your spirit to a world of extraordinary faith. We can't move mountains, but God can!

Discovering your God Moments of Unearned Blessing begins with the laying down of your pride. Contrary to our culture's invitation to buoy your self-esteem by rehearsing your own accomplishments, the God Moment Principle invites you to consider all the times you failed but were blessed anyway. The God Moment Principle requires you to take a long, honest look at your profound limitations. It begins with acknowledging all that you didn't do, couldn't do, and never will be able to do.

For example, a few questions worth asking: Who made you? Who decided when you would arrive on planet Earth? Who decided who your parents would be? Who made your mind? Did you know that research indicates you probably only use 2 to 5 percent of that wonderful brain of yours? How much do you really know? How did you learn it? Isn't almost all your knowledge built upon others' work? Are you prosperous? Where did your prosperity come from? Are you a self-made person? Really? No one helped you become who you are? What are your greatest blessings? Your children? Did you make them? Your work? Are you really indispensable?

Your Unearned Blessings may be tucked away in some unlikely spots. Look first to the places in life where you know your skills were inadequate. Reexamine the times in which you tried, failed, but were blessed anyway. Next, rethink the times of success. Look again at the things you are most proud of. Trace the blessing back to its earliest source. What you'll find, of course, is that "every good and perfect gift is from above" (James 1:17).

GOD MOMENTS MEMO

FINDING UNEARNED BLESSINGS

1. Reexamine the times your skills were inadequate but you were blessed anyway.
2. Dig through the treasure troves of your life. What has God given you in:
   - people you love and who love you;
   - places that have molded you;
   - provisions that came in timely or unexpected ways;
   - promotions you have been given;
   - privileges you have enjoyed.

My wife taught kindergarten for several years. One of the learning activities she employed was the time-tested game of Bingo. Letters and numbers—and prizes! It's a game of chance, as far as her kids knew. The teacher pulls numbers from a hat and the lucky one wins, right? Not exactly. Wanting every child to experience the thrill of winning, Anne would roam about the room looking for needed numbers on the cards of her winless kindergartners. Feigning a real draw, she would call out the necessary numbers so each child would get a chance to win. The unsuspecting child would holler, "Bingo! I did it! I won! Where's my prize?"

But a loving, sovereign teacher had orchestrated it all.

Your life hasn't been a series of accomplishments in which to boast. Your life hasn't been a random draw of luck and opportunity. A loving, sovereign God has been showering you with Unearned Blessings. God has orchestrated every good thing in your life.

As I think back on my conversation with A. C., perhaps I should have answered him differently. When he asked me why that man picked him out of the crowd for such a great job, maybe I should have just smiled and answered…"Bingo."

CHAPTER EIGHT

REVEALED
TRUTH

The Fourth Kind of God Moment

My beloved associate pastor has just left to plant our new "daughter church." So a few weeks ago, after twenty years of leadership and ministry in our midst, David Beaty and his wife Beth said good-bye during a morning worship service. Anyone who was in the room and breathing would have been moved. David's voice was steady at first, but when he said "Thank you for praying for our children," his voice broke. Only those who knew David and Beth more than seven years ago could grasp the full beauty and power of the memory that halted the young pastor's voice.

David and Beth met in our church. Blissfully married, they longed to bear children. They tried for five years. Anyone who has walked the road of infertility knows the uniqueness of that pain. Five years of yearning. Five years of medical treatment. Five years of disappointment.

Finally, Beth decided to forego any further fertility treatments and surrender the hope to God. Some women of the church approached the childless couple and promised to have a woman fasting and praying every day until they conceived a child. What followed was an unforgettable God Moment.

In January of 1992, despite her own battle with cancer, Pat Best was fasting and praying on behalf of the Beatys. A message burned in her heart. She approached David and Beth with the word she believed was from God. "I believe God has revealed that you'll have a baby next

February." The Scriptures remind us to weigh such messages carefully. The Beatys knew that loving people often give hopeful words rather than truly God-breathed words. Nonetheless, David and Beth felt a compelling encouragement in their hearts.

They charted out the calendar. A February birth would mean a May conception. The couple began believing that another Mother's Day would not go by without a conception. Imagine the anticipation that month. Imagine the disappointment. The month of May came and went like the other sixty months of hope and disappointment. No conception. Seemingly, no real word from God.

But in June, after more than five years of diligent effort, David and Beth Beaty conceived their first child. Words fall short of describing their joy at such a miracle. But how strange, they thought, that they would have been given such a distinct message from God that would be exactly one month off.

Late in Beth's pregnancy, Pat Best succumbed to cancer. The woman who had foreseen the miracle would witness the baby's birth only through the windows of heaven. From her heavenly mansion, I'm sure Pat was not surprised when David and Beth's baby arrived early. Anna Beaty was born in February. She's in kindergarten now. Her little brother, Matthew, is a preschooler.

So David Beaty's voice was tender but strong as he said good-bye to our congregation. But when he thought of the moment God spoke through a praying, fasting woman, he couldn't contain himself.

God didn't have to speak to *anyone* about the February baby, of course. The ladies still would have fasted and prayed. The Beatys still would have been overjoyed. Anna and Matthew could have been born right on time without any special message from God. But think of the difference it must have made in those parents' lives. The memory of the moment God spoke elicits more than tears in the young pastor's eyes—it evokes enormous confidence that God has a wonderful destiny for David and Beth's children.

Imagine the difference! Every exhausting late-night feeding…every Sunday dress spoiled by spit-up before stepping out the door…every earache visit to the doctor for amoxicillin…every baby food and diaper bill…is eased by the perspective of the God Moment. Every anxious moment is strangely calmed by the memory of God's voice. Every exasperating incident is lightened by the recollection of the revelation. Never will David and Beth roll their eyes in frustration and foolishly say, "Where did we get this child?" Instead, they'll forever have moisture in their eyes as they remember, "This child is the gift of God."

They experienced the unspeakable power of God's voice. Theirs was the God Moment of Revealed Truth. By remembering and sharing the moment God spoke, David and Beth regularly renew their confidence in God's calling for them to be parents.

Maybe God hasn't announced a miracle so dramatically to you. But, oh, how He has been speaking to you. Consider one woman's story...

"ARE YOU REALLY SPEAKING TO ME?"

"Are you really speaking to me?"

That was the gist of her remark. A thirsty Nazarene had asked a Samaritan woman for a drink of water. She was too amazed to answer the tired traveler directly, so she responded with an open mouth and an open question: "You are a Jew and I am a Samaritan woman. How can you ask me for a drink?" (see John 4:1–26).

She was stunned three times over. In the first place, men didn't speak to unknown women in the first-century Middle Eastern world. Secondly, a Jew certainly didn't speak to a Samaritan. Most Hebrews, in fact, would take time-costly detours to avoid traveling through Samaria. The Jewish people considered the Samaritans impure—a mixed breed who had intermarried with pagans. It was shocking for a Jewish man to speak to a Samaritan woman. Moreover, Samaritans had been deemed "unclean" by the Jewish leaders. Hence, for a rabbi to even drink from a Samaritan's cup would make him ceremonially unclean.

She couldn't believe her ears. "Are you really speaking to me?" Unwittingly, the woman at Jacob's well was asking the question that still lingers in most human hearts. "Are you really speaking to me, Lord?" It is a statement of yearning and disbelief. Yearning not to feel so vulnerable and alone. Disbelief that One so superior would overlook our failures and frailties and speak to us anyway.

Then, as now, Christ wanted His inquirer to hear His answer clearly: "Yes, I am speaking to you." He let her know by continuing His patient, winsome, and welcoming conversation with the adulterous woman who was, by any culture's standards, low in community esteem. He intrigued her with His promise: "Whoever drinks the water I give him will never thirst." He awed her with His knowledge: "You are right when you say you have no husband. The fact is, you have had five husbands, and the man you now have is not your husband." He taught her with His wisdom: "A time is coming when the true worshipers will worship the Father in spirit and truth." He captivated her with His claim: "I who speak to you am he."

If Christ desired to speak to a first-century Samaritan woman, then rest assured: He wants to speak to you.

The part of the story that intrigues me most is the part least noticed. It's what follows the dialogue between Jesus and the sinful woman: "Then, leaving her water jar, the woman went back to the town and said to the people, 'Come, see a man who told me everything I ever did'" (v. 28–29).

The woman had a moment with Christ—a God Moment. She would

GOD MOMENTS MEMO

THE WORDS OF JESUS TO THE SAMARITAN WOMAN
Intriguing Promise: "Whoever drinks the water I give him will never thirst."
Supernatural Insight: "You are right when you say you have no husband."
Divine Wisdom: "A time is coming when worshipers will worship the Father in spirit and truth."
Self-disclosure: "I who speak to you am [the Messiah]."
Jesus wanted to speak to the Samaritan woman. He wants to speak to you, too. The Lord will speak to you through the eternal promises of His word, through insights only He could know, through infinite wisdom for living, and through intimate self-revelation.

never forget it. She went to town and told everyone she knew. You can imagine what happened next.

"They came out of the town and made their way toward [Jesus]" (v. 30). Think about the impact. Jesus spoke to one woman and, suddenly, scores of people made their way to Christ. Later, the story tells us, "Many of the Samaritans from that town believed in him because of the woman's testimony, 'He told me everything I ever did'....And because of his words many more became believers" (v. 39, 41).

One conversation between Jesus Christ and a broken woman was enough to spark a full-scale revival in that Samaritan town. Such is the power of the God Moment of Revealed Truth. People who remember the sound of God's voice move forward with awesome confidence.

THE POWER OF PENTECOST

The Feast of Weeks takes its name from the command to "count off seven full weeks" after the Passover Sabbath (Leviticus 23:15). Its other name, Pentecost, likewise is labeled for the number of days between Passover and Pentecost (*penta* = "fifty"). This mandatory summer festival was joyful and expectant as worshipers presented offerings from the wheat harvest.

It was on this festive day, fifty days after the Passover Sabbath, that a wearied, worried band of disciples was transformed into a bold spiritual army destined to change the course of history.

> When the day of Pentecost came, they were all together in one place. Suddenly a sound like the blowing of a violent wind came from heaven and filled the whole house where they were sitting. They saw what seemed to be tongues of fire that separated and came to rest on each of them. All of them were filled with the Holy Spirit and began to speak in other tongues as the Spirit enabled them.
>
> Now there were staying in Jerusalem God-fearing Jews from every nation under heaven. When they heard this sound, a crowd came together in bewilderment, because each one heard them speaking in his own language. Utterly amazed, they asked: "Are not all these men who are speaking Galileans? Then how is it that each of us hears them in his own native language? Parthians,

Medes and Elamites; residents of Mesopotamia, Judea and Cappadocia, Pontus and Asia, Phrygia and Pamphylia, Egypt and the parts of Libya near Cyrene; visitors from Rome (both Jews and converts to Judaism); Cretans and Arabs—we hear them declaring the wonders of God in our own tongues!" Amazed and perplexed, they asked one another, "What does this mean?" (Acts 2:1–12)

The power of the Spirit rushed into their earthly house and into their human hearts. Pentecost would change the cowardly into the courageous. It would change the bashful into the bold. It would make the fainthearted fearless. Disciples from all over the known world, assembled for the Feast of Weeks, were changed forever by the awesome God Moment.

It was an indescribable moment. Like empty wells, the disciples suddenly were filled with living water. Ministry, prayer, and preaching suddenly became the joys of their lives. A man who denied Jesus three times was suddenly willing to die in His name. The worshipers were overwhelmed by the intoxicating, consuming presence of almighty God.

Embrace every aspect of that Pentecostal outpouring, but notice carefully the true focus of the moment. Celebrate the miraculous manifestations but don't miss the core of the event. It's the essence of Pentecost.

God spoke.

The blazing fire was leaping like tongues—the symbol of speech. The Galileans spoke by miraculous utterance not just so the crowd would be amazed, but so they would hear the Word of God in their own languages. Then Peter preached. The heart of Pentecost is God's voice to His people.[5]

Not surprisingly, the Word of God was the essence of the first Pentecost as well. Jewish tradition asserts that the first Pentecost took place as Israel gathered at Mt. Sinai to hear the law of God through Moses. There, at the first Festival of Weeks, "the Lord descended...in fire" (Exodus 19:18). The congregation at Sinai also saw the signs of a windstorm: "The people saw the thunder and lightning...and saw the mountain in smoke" (Exodus 20:18). The purpose of the Sinai gathering was for the people of God to hear the Word of God. God intended to reveal Himself, His wisdom, His promises, and His law to His people. Pentecost symbolizes God's desire to communicate His truth to all His people. It's the God Moment of Revealed Truth.

Revelation is, simply, an unveiling. It is the uncovering of what otherwise would remain hidden. It has been God's decision to not keep Himself hidden but to be seen and heard. He has revealed Himself in general ways…like the beauty of creation and His love toward all humanity. He has also chosen to reveal Himself in very specific ways…like a February baby announcement to the Beatys or a well-side conversation with a promiscuous Samaritan woman. The awesome good news of Pentecost is that God wants to speak to you personally. Like a curtain that lifts to reveal the actors behind it, Pentecost lifts the veil between you and God. The Lord's extraordinary gift is His own "Spirit of truth," who comes to us with the promise that "he will guide you into all truth" (John 16:13).

DISCOVERING YOUR GOD MOMENTS OF REVEALED TRUTH

You may be thinking, *But I've never had a miraculous message given to me. I've never heard the rushing wind or felt tongues of fire. I've never had a dramatic moment of revealed truth.*

GOD MOMENTS MEMO

THE FESTIVAL OF WEEKS (PENTECOST)
When? May–June, seven weeks or fifty days after the Passover Sabbath.
What? People assembled to hear God speak; a joyful festival presenting wheat harvest offerings.
Why? To remember how God has revealed Himself to His people.
Scriptures: Exodus 23:16a; Leviticus 23:15–16; see also Acts 2:1–12.
The God Moment: Revealed Truth.
The Spiritual Benefit: Renewed Confidence.

If those are your thoughts, I have good news. You don't have to experience wind or fire to hear from God. The earth doesn't have to shake and smoke needn't billow. In fact, God has spoken to you in a thousand different ways. He speaks through His Word, the Holy Bible. He speaks through a silent, inner witness of peace. He speaks as you talk and listen to Him in prayer. He speaks through divinely appointed conversations. He speaks through study. He speaks through flashes of insight. God loves to speak to His people. He loves speaking to *you.*

Acknowledge again that the Bible is God's voice to you and that it comes to life for Christians only because the Spirit illumines the Word of God. Rethink all the times in which you were led to helpful truth by what you called "a lightbulb going on." Reconsider the times in which you made a good decision because of what you called "intuition." Reassess the moments in which you did something well because you "just knew" it was the way to do it.

Have you ever had a verse of Scripture become especially meaningful at a crossroad in your life? Years ago, I was tempted to tone down my preaching because of one or two complainers. One afternoon during those discouraging days, I was stepping through my front door when I thought I heard the oddest conversation across the street: "Luke 12, verse 8!" I heard my neighbor say. I spun around in amazement. However, my neighbor was merely calling out a routine "good-bye" to a guest who was backing her car from the driveway. Mystified by what I thought I'd heard, I rushed to my Bible and wept as I read the verse: "I tell you, whoever acknowledges me before men, the Son of Man will also acknowledge him before the angels of God." Luke 12, verse 8. It was a verse I had read many times before, but suddenly God spoke it directly to my heart. He knew I needed the specific guidance and encouragement of that verse.

What Scriptures have greatly impacted you? Can you remember a specific moment? The circumstances that surrounded you on that day? When the Bible comes to life, it is a God Moment of Revealed Truth.

Take a moment to ponder the ways God speaks. Have you ever had wonderful "coincidences" through which you gained an important new insight? Has there ever been a person who spoke just the right word to you at just the right time to help you through a crisis?

Once you discover moments in which God has spoken to you, consider the vast ramifications of the God of the Universe speaking personally to you. The best way to fully appreciate your moments of Revealed Truth is to contemplate how one message from God can change the whole course of your life. A personal example comes to mind.

I met my wife in a Bible study at college. The first time we talked we stayed up all night. The exhilaration that grew in me was more than romantic love, it was the sense of God calling Anne and me to marriage. Through a strong, inner witness, I knew that God had spoken to me about my mate. Anne did, too. Wow—how can I describe how much my life has been blessed by this woman? If I contemplate a life without Anne, it means a life without the incredible love and joy she brings to each of my days. It means a life without little Bennett and Abigail. It probably means a whole different direction of ministry. I probably would have lived in a different part of the state or country, which would mean I would have missed all the life-changing relationships I now have. I probably wouldn't be pastoring my current flock. Do you see how expansive it gets? One God Moment of Revealed Truth sets a course of ever-expanding blessing.

Once you identify moments in which you can affirm that God revealed an important truth to you, ask yourself: *How would my life be different if God hadn't revealed that to me? What would I have missed if God had left me to my own wisdom?* Fill out the history of your life from those pivotal moments in which God directed your steps.

Let your growing awareness of God's voice in your past make you expectant of God's voice in the future. We do not have a God who hides; we have a God of revelation. Expect to hear Him speak. Expect moments of Revealed Truth.

A CAUTIONARY WORD...

Let me issue a word of caution here. God's voice is not the only voice seeking to gain your attention. The Scriptures teach that every child of God has a mortal enemy named Satan, who is primarily a deceiver. The enemy is crafty and will seek to lead you astray with all manner of distorted and perverted lies and half-truths. The primary way God speaks is through the Bible—the timeless, infallible Word of God. Measure all moments of

God's voice against the standard of the Scriptures.

God is never confusing. He will never lead you by fear or panic. Pray about any message you are not certain is from God. His voice always brings peace, never disorder. Remember that His Word expressly forbids consultation of any supernatural voice other than His own, through Jesus Christ. It's quite dangerous to use *Ouija* boards or to contact fortune-tellers, palm readers, or so-called psychics of any kind. Most are charlatans, but some do have a real, occultic connection to the powers

GOD MOMENTS MEMO

FINDING MOMENTS OF REVEALED TRUTH

1. Take an inventory of the good decisions you've made in your life. How did you know what was right or best? If it produced a godly blessing, it was God leading you.
   - When has a verse or theme of Scripture come alive to you?
   - When have you said, "A lightbulb just went on in my mind"?
   - When have you said, "It must have been intuition"?
   - When have you said, "I just knew what I was supposed to do"?

2. Take time to consider how one piece of revealed truth has impacted your whole life.
   - What relationships have you been led into?
   - What major decisions have resulted in far-reaching blessings?
   - What wisdom has molded the way you live?

3. Look at the significant areas of blessing in your life (e.g., your work, your family, your accomplishments). Trace the blessing back to its source. Usually, you'll find a moment of Revealed Truth at the blessing's birth.

of darkness. You don't need to spend your hard-earned money on a gimmicky phone call anyway. God wants to speak to you directly—and it's a toll-free call.

HOW REMEMBERING GOD MOMENTS OF REVEALED TRUTH BRINGS CONFIDENCE

In 1995, Laura Hull attended a retreat for our church's worship leaders. Interestingly, Laura was one of the few members invited who was not actually a music leader. Today, though, it's clear that God invited her to attend for a more important reason than worship leadership training. It was for a God Moment.

It was a peaceful time for Laura and her family. Though she had battled chronic colitis since 1984, she was enjoying an almost year-long period of relief from the terrible pain. Her husband, Tom, had been diagnosed in 1992 with Hodgkin's disease, but radiation had worked wonderfully and his scans were all clear. During this retreat in 1995, Laura never could have imagined how tough life would become in two short years. She never could have known the value of the God Moment.

The retreat leader, Dan Wilt, was led to sing a unique song for Laura. Though he had never met her before, Dan's music took on the quality of inspiration. It was a simple, warm, God-inspired song that warmed Laura's heart. Before I share the words, here's an important bit of background about Laura: All her life, she has loved sapphires. The sapphire is her birthstone. As a little girl, she would cherish gifts of imitation sapphires. She loves the blue stones more than diamonds. Dan Wilt, of course, didn't know this as he strummed his guitar and sang this spontaneous song for Laura Hull:

Precious sapphire, a stone, a gem
Bright blue sapphire, diadem
A jewel of great price
A stone of value
Immeasurable worth
That is your name.
Precious sapphire is your name.

Overjoyed, Laura drank in the words that she knew had been inspired by God. She felt treasured by God as she has treasured her own precious sapphires. Laura kept the memory of the song in her mind and a recording of it on cassette tape.

In February 1997, Laura experienced a severe recurrence of the colitis, which proved excruciating and unresponsive to traditional medications. Soon she would have multiple surgeries. In March 1997, her husband Tom was again diagnosed with cancer. He would receive chemotherapy from April through August. Hear Laura describe those days:

> There were days when all I could do was live. I was raising six- and eight-year-old girls, I was physically hurting as well as exhausted, and my ability to fight the good fight was often nil. There were times when I was so numb that I could not read the Word or even pray. I knew God was sovereign, but I needed to know He was HERE.

Laura found solitary moments in the car to be some of her loneliest, most vulnerable times. But she had a secret weapon against despair. She had a tool for hope. She had a God Moment memory—on tape!

So Laura played the God-given song over and over in her car. Every time she did, she remembered how God had spoken to her. She remembered that, despite her current pain, she was a precious sapphire in God's eyes. "Every time, my hope was restored," Laura says. "His grace would flood my spirit and thankfulness for His love would overwhelm me. The song was a tool He used to remind me of His unending mercy."

Everyone has a mental tape player in his or her mind. The songs you choose to play there will determine how you feel today and what you expect tomorrow. People who recognize and remember the moments of God's voice gain extraordinary confidence for living. Remembering the moments of Revealed Truth reassure you that you are not on your own and that God is in your life. Inwardly, we know how frail our own wisdom is. To live confidently, we need to know that a higher, wiser authority has spoken.

That's what happened to the disciples at Pentecost. God had spoken, so they preached with the memory of tongues of fire.

*W*hen you think about it, it was the God Moment of Revealed Truth that was pivotal throughout biblical history. The memory of God's voice kept Noah nailing planks—though the sky was blue. It kept Abraham counting stars and thinking about descendants—though his wife was over ninety. The memory of God's voice in a burning bush kept Moses returning to Pharaoh—though the oppression of the Hebrews only increased. The memory of God's voice kept Jeremiah and Isaiah preaching—though the nation wasn't repenting. It kept Nehemiah building—though his foes were laughing.

The memory of the angel's words to Mary ("You will give birth to a son...his kingdom will never end.") kept her close to her boy when the others had fled. The memory His Father's voice kept Jesus on the cross even as the mob baited Him to come down. The God Moment of Revealed Truth turned a band of cowardly disciples into an army that "turned the world upside down." The memory of God's voice on the Damascus road gave the apostle Paul confidence to preach boldly—even at risk of beatings, imprisonment, and death.

The God Moment of Revealed Truth can be just as powerful for you—today! The strain of your current adversity will tempt you to forget the sound of God's voice. In order to make sense of your present-day pain, you will be prone to look backward and doubt that God has actually spoken to you. But today's hardship does not erase yesterday's promise. No future emotional drought could take away the Samaritan woman's conversation with the Messiah who told her about "living water." No exasperating parenting dilemma could ever undo the moment God spoke to David and Beth Beaty about the blessing of a baby. No pain in her colon or chemotherapy for her husband could blot out the moment God told Laura Hull she was a precious sapphire.

No matter what this day presents, if you'll remember the moments God has revealed truth to you, you will find renewed confidence for living.

....

CHAPTER NINE

VALUABLE
ADVERSITY

The Fifth Kind of God Moment

t had a been a beautiful Thanksgiving eve. We heard from John Porter, who had been unresponsive in the intensive care unit for weeks but one day, miraculously, woke up. Laura Hull praised God as she described how she had survived a life-threatening intestinal obstruction while out of the country. James Wall, nearing eighty, told how he had breezed through open-heart surgery just a couple of weeks earlier.

They were all testimonies of completed God Moments. They were on the other side of their finish lines—already holding their trophies of praise. The testimonies were thrilling. But such victory reports can seem a bit distant for others in the pews. Most don't feel the joyous relief of having just crossed a finish line, for they are still running the race.

Why do we testify only from the moutaintops? How many praise reports do you hear from the desert? If we wait until we've arrived in the Promised Land before we announce our God Moments, we'll be silent most of the time.

That's why I'm glad Marion and Bridgette Blackwell spoke. They weren't living yet in the land of milk and honey, but the promise of grace was living in them. Future victory was assuring them while their race was still being run. Their testimony would reveal the most often overlooked God Moment.

"We have been in the desert," the man of God announced to our

Thanksgiving service crowd. "We're still in a desert. And I want to thank God for what He's doing.

"As most of you know, my wife has been battling a life-threatening kidney ailment. We've seen God at work. She's much better. Thankfully, she will not need a kidney transplant or regular dialysis. We're still waiting for her complete healing."

Bridgette was just as honest. "This hasn't been just any desert—it's been the Sahara! Sometimes it has been all I could do to just cry out, 'Son of David, have mercy.' But I have felt the Lord's presence most near when I have been at my lowest. He has taken away my fear. I have known His love. In the midst of it all, I have been deeply blessed."

Marion spoke again. "As many of you know, six months ago I lost my job. I was downsized. But I was strangely prepared. Amazingly, two nights before I was told about the downsizing I had a vivid dream. In that dream, I saw my boss call me into his office. I sat down and listened to him say, 'Marion, I have to let you go. It's a corporate downsizing.' Still in the dream, I asked, 'Have I done anything wrong?' He answered, 'No, you've done a great job.' I left his office. The dream was over and I woke up.

"Two days later I went to work as usual and lived out the dream. My boss called me in. I sat down. He said, 'I have to let you go.' I asked if I had done anything wrong. He said, 'No, it's a corporate downsizing. You've done a great job.'

"The dream had prepared me. I think my boss had a harder time with it than I did. I found myself reassuring *him*, 'It's all right, boss. I'm going to be just fine.'

"It's been six months now. My severance package is running out. I still don't have a job. But I know God has a purpose behind all this. He has a great job for me somewhere. I'm sure He'll show it to me soon."

Marion looked at his children on the third pew. That's when his voice broke. With unashamed emotion, the steady man of faith wept as he declared an astounding truth: "I can honestly say that this has been the best year of my life." He squeezed his wife's hand. "My wife and I are more in love than we were when we were first married. And these months of unemployment have given me the chance to spend quantity time with my kids." He looked at them. "I had forgotten just how much I love you guys. I have loved every minute with you."

Then Marion concluded, "We might have been in a desert, but I wouldn't trade this year for all the world."

He was in the desert, but he wouldn't trade it for the lushest land of milk and honey. Why? Because he had discovered new intimacy amidst the agony. He had found something of infinite value in the midst of temporary adversity.

Marion has a fine job now. Bridgette's health is good. They're not in that desert anymore. But if you asked them, they wouldn't choose to undo their trial. They'll always treasure their God Moment of Valuable Adversity.

So did Joseph.

*J*acob's favorite boy was despised by his jealous older brothers. They hated his special coat and they hated him. Of course, that hatred was fertile soil for the seed of betrayal. The brothers plotted to kill him but instead decided to make a quick buck. They sold him to Midianite merchants who, in turn, hocked him to an Eyptian official named Potiphar.

Hated. Betrayed. Abused. Twice sold. For Joseph, it was a desert. And it was about to become hotter.

Potiphar's wife falsely accused the man of God. Joseph was thrown into prison for two years. Two years to wonder what had happened to his dream…to be tempted to give up on God…to taste the dust of a desert. But that's not how Joseph did his time. For him, it was two more years of hoping. Two more years of training. Two more years of growing stronger in his faith.

When Joseph interpreted Pharoah's dream, he became an "instant" success. Everyone in Egypt was asking, "Who's the new guy?" Suddenly Joseph was exalted to the place of second-in-command of all Egypt. By God's irrevocable plan, the Word that was spoken to Joseph in a boyhood dream came true. His brothers, desperate for food, unknowingly bowed before the new leader. When Joseph finally unveiled his identity to his hungry brothers, emotion overtook him:

> Then Joseph could no longer control himself before all his attendants, and he cried out, "Have everyone leave my presence!" So

there was no one with Joseph when he made himself known to his brothers. And he wept so loudly that the Egyptians heard him. (Genesis 45:1–2)

If you listen closely, you can hear the sound of his wails. Those are not the moans of an angry brother; they are the sobs of a man in love with God. Listen again. Those are not the cries of a vengeful sibling; they are the inward groans of gratitude too deep for words. Those wails are the expression of awesome praise to the God who snatches out unspeakable good from the jaws of unthinkable evil.

Joseph's tears were an eruption of thanks for the surprising value of adversity. He cried that day over the truth he would later exclaim to his fearful brothers:

"Don't be afraid. Am I in the place of God? You intended to harm me, but God intended it for good to accomplish what is now being done, the saving of many lives. So then, don't be afraid. I will provide for you and your children." And he reassured them and spoke kindly to them. (Genesis 50:19–21)

Joseph was full of blessing instead of curses because his spirit was full of the God Moment of Valuable Adversity. Instead of looking backward and brooding over humiliating moments in a pit or "wasted" days in prison, Joseph's mind was fixed on the activity of God amidst his difficulties. He remembered the events of his life only in the context of God's supernatural intervention. He had love, joy, and peace only because he recognized and rehearsed his God Moments.

Joseph had been in places nobody wants to go. In the shaft of rejection. In the shackles of bondage. In the stockade of obscurity. But out of places where Joseph never wanted to be, God moved him into a place greater than he had ever hoped for. Sometimes the very thing we most want to avoid becomes the womb of what we most want to attain. God never wastes adversity. Our most difficult moments may also be some of our greatest God Moments.

It was also true for Abraham. The man who God promised would be a father of a nation "obeyed and went, even though he did not know where he was going" (Hebrews 11:8). The "father of a nation" walked in a desert of childlessness for years after the promise. He learned faith.

It was true for David. The obscure, overlooked shepherd who, though anointed, hid in caves from the lunatic King Saul. He learned humility.

It was true for Paul. The prideful persecutor of Christians was blinded on the Damascus road. The man who would change the world with his preaching was pitifully led by the hand for three days of humiliation. He learned how strength is perfected.

It was true for Jesus. The moment of His driest desert is the moment of eternal saving power. The moment of greatest humiliation, the Cross, is the greatest God Moment of all time.

THE MARK OF MATURITY: FINDING VALUE IN ADVERSITY

Put yourself in the place of the four-year-olds in a remarkable psychological study begun in the 1960s. A nice, smiling man gives you a plump white marshmallow to eat. Your eyes grow wide, your toddler mouth waters, and you get ready to stuff it into your little jaws. But wait! Here comes another option. The nice man informs you that if you will wait while he runs an errand, he'll give you *two* marshmallows when he gets back.

What do you do? Seize the day like the other kids are doing and stuff that marshmallow in your mouth? Or do you wait it out for the promise of *two* marshmallows?

To wait it out means adversity. It means not having what you want to have. It means watching others have a feast while you're in a famine. It means trusting a promise while others are eating a treat. One thing is for sure: Your four-year-old mouth will never wait for the two marshmallows unless your four-year-old brain believes that sometimes a greater gain is worth a momentary pain.

Amazingly, some four-year-olds in the experiment believed in the value of temporary adversity and waited it out. While most toddlers grabbed the one marshmallow, some children found a way to tough it out for fifteen minutes until the experimenter returned. They covered their eyes, talked to themselves, played games, or tried to go to sleep. After their momentary adversity, the persevering toddlers received *double the pleasure* of the others.

But the real value of their patience wasn't discovered until the experiment was completed twelve to fourteen years later.

The ones who had endured the fifteen-minute adversity as toddlers were, as teenagers, dramatically better adjusted than their marshmallow-grabbing counterparts. The wait-for-the-marshmallow crowd was "more socially competent, personally effective, self-assertive, and better able to cope with the frustrations of life. They were less likely to go to pieces, freeze, or regress under stress...they were confident, trustworthy, and dependable."[6] Even more remarkably, the kids who waited for the two-marshmallow reward scored an average of 210 points higher on their SAT tests than those who eagerly wolfed down the single marshmallow.

It's about more than marshmallows—it's about a rule of life: *The way you view your adversity today determines the height to which you will rise tomorrow.*

God doesn't just *sustain* us amidst adversity, He *prepares* us. The Lord doesn't just give us strength to carry on when we have no marshmallow— He uses the no-marshmallow moments to prepare a two-marshmallow blessing!

THE FEAST OF TABERNACLES

The Lord said to Moses, "Say to the Israelites: 'On the fifteenth day of the seventh month the Lord's Feast of Tabernacles begins, and it lasts for seven days.... This is to be a lasting ordinance for the generations to come.... Live in booths for seven days: All native-born Israelites are to live in booths so your descendants will know that I had the Israelites live in booths when I brought them out of Egypt.'" (Leviticus 23:33, 41–43)

The final annual feast of Israel takes its name from the Hebrew word *(Sukkot)* that describes the leafy, three-sided huts that God's people inhabited for seven days. The construction and occupation of the "booths" reminded Hebrew families that they once lived in the wilderness. The humble lodgings compelled them to acknowledge that they had traveled through a desert in order to reach a promised land.

Like the wilderness originals, the mandated festival huts were humble, temporary dwellings symbolizing the humility and adversity of desert times. Yet, at the same time, the unpretentious dwellings reminded them that God cared for His people deeply and practically while they wandered in their wilderness. The Lord provided for His people. He rained manna on the ground—daily bread. He issued drink from the rock—living water. Though they endured the adversity of the desert, God was with them.

So the Feast of Tabernacles was an occasion for joy. Because the final harvest had been gathered, the festival was sometimes referred to as the Feast of Ingathering and eventually came to be known as The Season of Our Joy. Like the hearty laughter at a party on a Friday night after a long week's work, the final feast was celebrated with the lightheartedness of laborers at rest. Tabernacles took place amidst the prosperity of an abundant final harvest.

Do you see the irony—and the impact? When life was its richest and easiest, all Israelites were required to abandon the comfort of their fine homes and crowd into temporary, leafy huts. When life presented its least adversity, every Hebrew family had to move into a blatantly adverse circumstance. Once the Hebrew family entered the booth, they took time to reflect on the nature of the little hut that would be their home for the holiday. The Jewish father followed the developed liturgy in which he reminded his children that:

> A man must not put his trust in the size or strength or salutary conveniences of his house, even though it be filled with the best of everything; nor should he rely upon the help of any man, even though he be the lord of the land. But let him put his trust in Him Whose word called the universe into being."[7]

The hut symbolizes that our security is only in God—the One in whom we "live and move and have our being" (Acts 17:28).

The blessedness of your life is not measured by the wealth you've acquired. The safety of your life is not defined by the extravagance of your house. The hope of your life is not rooted in the comfort of your circumstances. The joy of your life is not founded on the ease of your situation. Your blessing is in God. Your security is in God. Your hope is in God. Your joy is in God.

Three years ago, a huge hurricane ripped through my North Carolina

GOD MOMENTS MEMO

THE FEAST OF TABERNACLES
When? The last of the fall feasts, September–October.
What? A week celebrating the final harvest; living in booths; offering sacrifices.
Why? To remember that God is our dwelling place and that we can be blessed amid difficult circumstances.
Scriptures: Leviticus 23:33–43; Numbers 29:12–13;
(see also John 7:2, 37).
The God Moment: Valuable Adversity.
The Spiritual Benefit: Perseverance.

neighborhood. Trees crushed roofs, blocked streets, and severed power lines. Our peaceful, clean neighborhood was suddenly chaotic. No telephones. No water. No electricity. No cable TV!

Isn't it amazing how people can cooperate when there is a common enemy to fight? The adverse circumstances brought people off their couches and out from in front of the TV. Men shared ladders and chain saws. Women shared food. Strangers who had lived next to each other for years suddenly became friends. The owners of four-wheel-drive vehicles shuttled people about. It was beautiful. A *community* was born. People practiced love in the most tangible ways.

After a few weeks the roads were cleared, the power was restored, the TVs were glowing again, the couch potatoes were replanted—and people became strangers, like before. I remember my associate, who lived in our neighborhood, musing, "Oh, that we could just have another hurricane...."

Sometimes it's not until everything is stripped away that we discover the best things in life like love, community, and joy. Such was the Feast of Tabernacles—a week to lay aside the nonessentials in order to reclaim the essentials. The wise Hebrew father saw it and taught it: The hut of humility is not a curse, it is a gift.

UNCOVERING YOUR GOD MOMENTS
OF VALUABLE ADVERSITY

1. Review your past for moments of adversity that saved you from worse destruction.

The Scriptures tell us that pride precedes our worst times. "Pride goes before destruction, a haughty spirit before a fall" (Proverbs 16:18). Therefore, if God lets you get humiliated, He's doing you a great favor!

Have you ever seen the dunking booth at the fair? I saw one up close last weekend—real close. I was in it. About fifty times, I think.

A dunking booth is a contraption that perches a person behind a cage on a trap seat above a pool of water. Its mechanism connects to a target on the side. People pay money to throw balls at the target. When the target is hit, the person behind the cage is dunked. The idea is for the guy in the booth to taunt, mock, and egg on the throwers so they will get madder and madder—and spend more money trying to dunk him.

In my case, it was sort of hard thinking up ways to taunt members of my own congregation. What was I supposed to say? "Hey, you're so ugly that it's a good thing God looks upon the heart!" Or what about, "With ability like yours, thank God you're saved by grace, not works!" Anyway, you get the idea.

One time at the Myrtle Beach pavilion I saw the most obnoxious, objectionable, prideful man in a dunking booth I'd ever seen before or since. He spotted a man in a cowboy hat and started ridiculing the man's wife: "Hey, lady, you've got one of those hourglass figures—except the sand has all run to the bottom! Ha, ha, ha!" The man in the cowboy hat didn't laugh. In fact, I thought the cowboy was going to climb over the cage and dunk the guy permanently.

The only thing that saved the dunking booth guy was a cool teenager with a good arm. Right about when the cowboy had reached the boiling point, the teenager zinged a fastball smack onto the target and *SPLASH!*— the obnoxious one swallowed some water and some pride. The cowboy laughed and decided to let his mocker live.

Sometimes the best thing that can happen to you is to get knocked off your high perch. I look at it this way: God has a good arm, and sometimes He'll dunk you to save you.

When the Israelites were headed out of Egypt toward the Promised Land, they took the long route through the desert instead of the shortcut through Philistine country. And it was God's fault.

> When Pharaoh let the people go, God did not lead them on the road through the Philistine country, though that was shorter. For God said, "If they face war, they might change their minds and return to Egypt." So God led the people around by the desert road toward the Red Sea. (Exodus 13:17–18)

Later, Moses reiterated the point: "Remember how the Lord your God led you all the way in the desert these forty years, to humble you" (Deuteronomy 8:2).

I once read about a guy who bought some new silk pajamas that he planned to take on an adulterous fling. When he was trying them on in his bathroom, he slipped, fell, and cracked his head on the tile floor. A couple of days later he awoke in the hospital. His mistress, who was infuriated at being stood up, called the whole scandalous relationship off. Now that's what I call a moment of Valuable Adversity!

Review your life. Look at the moments of adversity along the way. Can you identify times in which a temporary season of adversity saved you from a potentially worse adversity? Can you think of times in which a temporary fall, though humiliating, saved you from a permanent fall?

Keep in mind, the Bible clearly teaches that God is not the author of evil: "When tempted, no one should say, 'God is tempting me.' For God cannot be tempted by evil, nor does he tempt anyone" (James 1:13). We're not looking for ways God has sent evil into our lives, for He doesn't do that. Instead, we're searching for ways in which God used *the enemy's* evil intent to protect us from something worse.

Recall even your driest deserts when you have felt bereft of all normal comfort and security. Desert times make your soul feel parched. How have your desert times made you grow spiritually? Consider even your most acute, painful moments: Loss of a relationship. Loss of a job. Loss of a dream. Do you recall some moments when the pain felt so great you could hardly bear it? What emerged on the other side? New relationships?

New intimacy? New perspectives? Consider also all the moments you thought were failures. Can you remember any moments of failure which, though painful at the time, saved you from taking a wrong path?

2. Try to recall ways in which moments of adversity prepared you to receive a greater blessing.

Fallen evangelist Jim Bakker describes the day his son Jamie visited him in prison:

> The longer we talked, the more open we both became with each other. He spoke straightforwardly of his involvement with drugs, alcohol, and sex. I told him candidly and in detail of the events leading up to my tryst with Jessica Hahn. I tried to explain to him again how I had lost PTL. We talked hour after hour. We laughed a lot. We cried a bit. And, for the first time in his sixteen years, Jamie and I spent one entire day alone together. The irony was not lost upon me, that *it took me going to prison before I could spend the day with my son*, giving him my undivided attention."[8]

Deep humiliation welcomes the greatest blessings in life. Why? Because "God opposes the proud *but gives grace to the humble*" (James 4:6, emphasis added). When the disciples asked Jesus who was the greatest in the kingdom, He pointed to a humble little child. Paul described the same truth when he said he had discovered God's strength most perfectly amidst personal weakness.

It's a simple principle. God blesses us only as much as He can without us becoming prideful. The less likely we are to take credit for the blessings, the more likely God is to grant them. Every deeply anointed man or woman I know has endured a season of humiliation in the desert. Indeed, as I reflect on my own life, I can see now that every major blessing has been preceded by a season of humiliation:

...When my parents' marriage broke, my fourth-grade heart broke. But that was the desert that brought me to God in the first place.

...When I was called into the ministry, I wept for hours over my sin. Like Isaiah, I felt undone. But that was the desert that determined my destiny.

...When I began in the ministry, I started in utter obscurity. But that was the desert that taught me to love people.

…When we wanted a child, we tried for over a year. But that was the desert that made us such grateful parents.

I'm in a desert now. My wife's sister faces chemotherapy again today. My dad is scheduled for a brain biopsy tomorrow. The weight of life's difficulties is collapsing on me—but I feel myself falling more in love with Jesus Christ. I've come to get almost excited over humiliating desert experiences because they cause me to hunger more deeply for knowledge of the supremacy and sufficiency of Christ. The moments of adversity form the womb of life's deepest blessing.

Think back to the times you were humbled. Think of the times when you felt like a flop. Don't hesitate to drudge up your most embarassing moments. Then consider what happened in the next season of your life. It may not have been immediate. It may not have been overt. But if you ponder it carefully, you'll probably discover a rich blessing on the other side of your humiliation. Those subsequent blessings turn your humble times into the God Moments of Valuable Adversity.

HOW MOMENTS OF VALUABLE
ADVERSITY BUILD PERSEVERANCE

Like me, you might be in the desert now. You might look at others' mansions and wonder why you are stuck in a leafy hut. Life can get dry as dust, can't it? The deserts of life make us wonder if there is any water left. Adversity can get so strong that we wonder how we'll make it.

The God Moments principle provides a big part of the answer. When we find ourselves hurting, lonely, or thirsting, the natural tendency is to look forward. When will this agony end? What does tomorrow hold? Such forward, hypothetical thinking can actually exacerbate our current anguish because we don't know the future. We have no idea how long a desert will last or how our circumstances will work out.

What we do know is the past. The person who successfully remembers the value of yesterday's adversity can rehearse those memories in the midst of a current desert. The commemorative process reassures us amidst the desolation: "I've been in a dry place before and God took me through—there's no reason why He can't take me through this one, too."

That's the Hebrew memory in the hut.

*M*arion and Bridgette sat down. The Thanksgiving service was drawing to a close. I didn't look around to see if everyone else was crying, but I gave myself time to wipe away my own tears. Theirs had been the best testimony of the night. And it had not been spoken from a mountaintop, but from a leafy hut in a desert.

....

CHAPTER TEN

THE CONNECTION
KEYSTONE

Hindsight Isn't Always 20/20

*T*he old saying isn't always true. Hindsight isn't always 20/20. When it comes to God Moments, you might not see your past clearly. We can have some incredible, even miraculous, moments that we never connect to God or His purposes. But God wants His people to see their lives linked with His power and plan.

As Moses forecast the Passover, he made the link: "There will be loud wailing throughout Egypt.... But among the Israelites not a dog will bark at any man or animal. Then you will know that the LORD makes a distinction between Egypt and Israel" (Exodus 11:6–7). In other words, the events that are about to transpire will be unmistakably connected to God's saving purposes. Later, the Lord adds these intriguing words: "The blood will be a sign *for you* on the houses where you are" (Exodus 12:13, emphasis added). The blood wasn't a sign for God, it was for the Hebrews. It was so *the people* would make the connection. The blood would prove that the Passover was no random moment of chance. Rather, it proved the Passover to be a God Moment.

Our hindsight isn't always 20/20.

Jacob was a man unaware that his life was connected to heaven. He was clever. He was deceptive. And he was a winner. But Jacob didn't know the source of his success. He knew he had stolen his father's blessing, but he had no idea how deep the blessing would run. He knew he had received unmerited favor, but he had no idea how irreversibly his life had become linked to the purposes of God.

After stealing his older brother's blessing from their father, Jacob fled his brother's wrath. Rebekah, Jacob's mother and co-conspirator, had urged her favorite boy to leave town until Esau's fury subsided. "Why should I lose both of you in one day?" she reasoned (Genesis 27:45). So "Jacob left Beersheba and set out for Haran" (Genesis 28:10).

As far as Jacob knew, it was an ordinary and necessary trip to get away from his angry brother. Nothing more, nothing less, was on his mind when he stopped at nightfall, put a stone under his head, looked at the stars, and fell asleep. He was expecting nothing more than a night's rest. Instead, his life was changed forever by a dream.

Have you ever noticed that some of the most powerful revelations of our lives sneak up on us in the midst of ordinary activity? God loves to catch us by surprise, doesn't He? When we're in the middle of the third load of laundry...or in a hallway conversation at work...or when a frustrating toddler says something irresistibly cute...God speaks. Just when we begin to feel like we're completely on our own, we discover we're not. Suddenly, amidst the mundane, we realize we are connected to the eternal. Suddenly, a God Moment. That's what happened to Jacob.

Here's how the Scripture recounts the life-changing dream:

> He saw a stairway resting on the earth, with its top reaching to heaven, and the angels of God were ascending and descending on it. There above it stood the Lord, and he said: "I am the Lord, the God of your father Abraham and the God of Isaac. I will give you and your descendants the land on which you are lying. Your descendants will be like the dust of the earth, and you will spread out to the west and to the east, to the north and to the south. All peoples on earth will be blessed through you and your offspring. I am with you and will watch over you wherever you go, and I will bring you back to this land. I will not leave you until I have done what I have promised you." (Genesis 28:12–15)

Jacob thought he was on an ordinary journey, but he discovered that it was extraordinary. He thought he was treading commonplace turf, but he found it to be holy ground. He thought he had cleverly grasped his brother's inheritance, but learned that he had been inseparably grasped by almighty Jehovah's enduring promises.

He saw a stairway stretching from earth to heaven. Angels of God were ascending and descending the stairway. Suddenly Jacob was stricken with a transforming revelation. His earthly existence was invisibly linked with heaven. He was connected to God. The events of his life were connected with God's purposes. He had been seeing only the earthly side of it. His eyes suddenly were opened to a whole new heavenly world. "When Jacob awoke from his sleep, he thought, 'Surely the LORD is in this place, and I was not aware of it'" (Genesis 28:16).

A sudden dawning. A lifted veil. A paradigm shift. A whole new way of viewing life. That's what happens when God Moments come crashing in. As you begin to discover God in your past, you, too, will say to yourself, *Surely the Lord is in this place, and I was not aware of it.*

When you discover the presence of the heavenly Father where you previously assumed yourself to be alone, you've apprehended the first keystone to God Moments:

Connection.

A contemporary illustration will help us grasp this truth. One day, a woman in my congregation suddenly realized her life was connected to the father she had always assumed wasn't there. Listen to her miracle. Watch for the life change a *connection* can make.

DISCOVERING THE LOVE OF A FATHER

Hannah has just returned from her father's funeral. She sits in my study with bewildered tears that betray the softness of her soul. Hannah is a never-married attorney who works hard but doesn't live for her work—she lives for the Lord. We have prayed together before about life, about joy, about pain, about dreams. But this day is different. I can see it in her tears and hear it in her voice. Hannah is wrestling with something she has never wrestled with before.

She describes the events of the past weeks. "I get a phone call, Pastor, out of the blue...

"'Is this Hannah?'

"'Yes, this is Hannah,' I say.

"'I'm sorry to tell you that your father is dead. We have him in our morgue.'

"It was just that plain, Pastor. Just that quick. The caller didn't elaborate. She gave me no details. Just, *wham!* No one was with me. I didn't know what to think or do. I was just stunned." Hannah pauses, shifts in her chair, then continues. "At least I had spoken with him recently."

The tears flow freely. "You see, Pastor, my father left home when I was little. He hated my mother. He really hated her. And he didn't want anything to do with me, either." What she shares next breaks her voice—and my heart. "When my parents split up, neither of them wanted me. I've always believed my father hated me."

You can imagine her pain. No memories of being tickled by a laughing dad. No warm recollection of gentle squeezes after bedtime stories. No father to confide in after a difficult day at school. No spiritual head to teach her how to pray. No remembrance of a tender warrior to defend her in her times of need. Hear the anguish of her words again: *"I've always believed my father hated me."*

"He's never provided for me—*never,*" Hannah continues, now with a subtle flash of anger behind her tears. "He couldn't save any money, and he never gave me or Mom anything. When I began making plans for his burial, I called his girlfriend to see if she knew of any provision he had left for his burial. There wasn't any. I was going to have to do it all by myself. It wasn't just the money, Pastor. It was the pain of realizing that, even in his death, he had been selfish. It was like the final blow of rejection toward me. He was hurting me even from the grave. But he was my father, and I needed to give him a proper burial."

Hannah's voice changes. Some new information is about to emerge. "But while I was making his burial preparations, I discovered that he had a safe-deposit box at the bank. After quite a bit of effort, I was allowed to check the contents of the box."

Hannah stops and stares at me like a deer in headlights, frozen with the confusion of strange new light. "Pastor," she confides, "Dad had a little insurance policy. Not a lot, but something. I was the sole beneficiary. And he had several thousand dollars cash in the box. With it he had left a note to me. The money was for *me.*"

Hannah places her hand over her heart. "For *me,* Pastor. I don't understand. He could have left that money to his girlfriend or someone else, but he left it all for *me.* And he had a coin collection that was his pride and joy. That was in the box—*for me, too.*"

For a moment we sit silently, pondering, praying. Finally she asks, "What does it mean, Pastor?"

I pray for God's guidance and weigh my words carefully. "I think it means, Hannah, that your father loved you. Despite the way he seemed to you while he lived, in his death your father revealed his heart. If he really hated you, he wouldn't have left you his treasures, would he? He left you everything precious to him. It wasn't a lot, but it was all he had. People don't leave their treasures to people they hate—they leave them to people they love. Maybe he didn't know how to show it. Maybe he was so mad at your mother that he couldn't get close to you. Maybe he was hurting so badly inside that he couldn't find a way to let his love out toward you. But the lockbox means you were the last and most important thing on his mind. The lockbox means you were the most precious thing in his life.

"What it all means, Hannah, is that your father didn't hate you—he loved you. The father you thought to be so distant was always invisibly connected to you."

She's silent long enough to let the words sink in. "My father loved me?" Again, Hannah ponders the revelation. "I don't even know how to absorb it."

"It's going to take a while, Hannah." I try to prepare her. "You're going to have to rethink and reinterpret a lot of the events and conversations of your life. All the places of pain and loneliness in your past in which you assumed your father hated you must be revisited. You've just been given an incredible gift. You now have the opportunity to remember your life differently. The events won't change. But the way you feel about the events will change. You've had a father who loved you—you just didn't know it. Now that you do know it, it changes everything."

We're both smiling as we walk to the door. Hannah's face is glowing. "My father loved me—*my father actually loved me!*"

FILTERED MEMORIES

Though Hannah had remembered only the heartache of distance from her father, that day she discovered a link. It was like a Jacob's ladder from her own soul to her dad's. Where she had assumed there was no connection, she discovered an undeniable bond. Where she had seen no provision, she discovered cash in a safe-deposit box. Where she had seen no affection, she discovered hidden love.

Fortunately, God is different from Hannah's father. God knows how to demonstrate His love and has always been at work showing it. But in our walk with God, we are a lot like Hannah with her dad. The pain of circumstances, the scattered feelings of abandonment, and the blinding force of our spiritual enemy can close our eyes to the love of our heavenly Father.

This spiritual reality is corroborated by medical evidence. Scientific research proves that our brains filter memories, sometimes causing them to be inaccurate. Interest, emotion, and distortion all can affect our memory.

For example, one of my dearest memories is of our family's summer vacations at Myrtle Beach. Every year we spent a delicious week at the Driftwood Motel. The memories are so powerful that, even as I sit in front of my computer, I can close my eyes and smell the unique aroma of salt air wafting up from the beach dunes to the public rinsing shower. I can easily hear, in my mind's ear, the clack of the scuffling palm branches adjacent to the open-sided, cold-water shower. I can see the panorama of the Grand Strand Beach as it opens before a little child who has just stepped through the threshold of the covered entryway. I can feel the fresh shower water and the residue of ocean water mingle and run down my face, trickling a salt flavor to my lips.

I remember the sights, smells, and sounds of that particular point behind the Driftwood Motel because it was the entry point to the greatest playland of my boyhood. A never-ending sandbox. A never-ending wave ride. A world away from the world. A place where life was measured not by accomplishments but by relationships. The little showering spot was a place of significant passage for me. It represented some of my deepest delights— fun, camaraderie, playfulness, joy, lasting relationships, freedom.

But imagine visiting the beach shower just once thirty years ago, and only because you were walking down the beach and you stopped to visit a friend who was staying at the Driftwood. You stepped through, rinsed the sand off your feet, and proceeded to make your visit. Of course, you wouldn't even remember the silly old showering spot as I do. To you it was meaningless. You used it and went on. You don't remember its smells or sights or sounds. You attach no meaning to the spot.

The meaning you attach to a moment will determine its weight upon your memory. Psychiatrist Frank Minirth describes it this way:

> Interest…is a major factor in how the brain will treat information, dismissing some elements and retaining others. Emotion is another. Memories and mood feed on each other. A positive mood creates positive memories, and a negative mood creates negative memories…. Interest and emotions influence what the brain sifts out to save and how it will save it.[9]

This truth is pivotal to harnessing your God Moments. It explains the reason you have kept certain powerful God Moment memories and missed others. For example, God might have spoken to you in a powerful way in the midst of an emotional ebb in your life. But because of your depressive mood during that season, you tended to overlook all the truly positive voices in your life—especially God's. A time in which you felt unconnected to God is actually a time in which your interest or emotion predisposed you to shut your ears to His reassuring voice.

DISTORTED MEMORIES

Medical studies have revealed another way in which your brain filters long-term memories: a phenomenon researchers call *distortion*. Your brain can actually distort a memory because of what you *expected* to experience. You can, unconsciously, change a memory's shape to fit a shape already preconceived by your experience or environment.

Researchers once explored this tendency by telling a Northwest Indian culture story to non-Indians. Three days later, when the non-Indians were asked to repeat the story, their minds distorted the story in accord with their own culture. The non-Indian subjects omitted certain details that didn't seem to fit culturally and added details that were culturally relevant to them, but not to the Indian culture from which the story arose. The subjects had no idea that they were adding or changing the story. They were remembering the story and relating it as faithfully as they knew how.[10]

Perhaps the most obvious way distortion affects our memories of God

Moments is in our lives before we gave our hearts to God. If you are a follower of Jesus Christ today, there probably was a time in which your eyes were blind to the love of the Savior (unless you are one of those blessed ones like Ruth Graham or my wife, both of whom declare that they can't remember a time when they didn't love Jesus). Any time in your life in which you had not yet believed that God was real, that He sent His Son to die for you, and that He wanted to be active in your life, was a time in which you were distorting memories of God Moments. God was there protecting you, speaking to you, preparing you. Christ has been with you from the time you were knit together in your mother's womb. The Holy Spirit has been wooing you, calling you, loving you. But chances are, you've distorted all those pre-Christian memories. Imagine the God Moments you can reclaim with a simple reexamination of your pre-Christian life!

Christians distort memories of God Moments, too. By far the most prevalent example is betrayed by our unbelief. If you believe God's power was reserved for the Israelites to escape the Egyptian enemy but not for the modern Christian to escape the diabolic enemy, then you'll distort your God Moments of Amazing Rescue into moments of luck or good fortune. If you think God spoke at Pentecost but not in your prayer closet, then you'll distort the God Moments of Revealed Truth into moments of intuition or personal wisdom. If you think Jesus healed lepers on the streets of Jerusalem but not cancer patients in modern hospitals, you'll be thankful for chemotherapy and doctors but not for God's hand at work. It's always beautiful to watch a Christian open his eyes and heart to the present-day miracles of God. With wide-eyed spiritual wonder, they exclaim: "I never knew God was so good.... I feel like I've stepped into a whole new world. Everything looks new to me!"

If you are in a tough place in life right now, pay special attention to the phenomenon of memory distortion. It might be robbing you of the very God Moment power you need to lift you from a deep pit of despair. Memory distortion might be stealing the very light you need to dispel your current darkness.

One of the best Christian psychologists I know, Michael Quirk, Ph.D., further explained the distortion process for me. "People tend to re-create their past memories to match their current pain," Quirk noted. "In other words, if someone is depressed today, he will seek reasons for his depression in his past because he wants to 'make sense' of his current emotional distress."

For example, if you feel sad today, you'll probably look for reasons for your sadness. Not knowing any immediate, rational reasons to be sad, you will probably begin rethinking your past. You'll eventually reinterpret and distort memories to explain your sadness. You may find yourself saying things like, "I'm always getting bad breaks" or "Nothing good seems to happen to me."

Of course, such distorted thinking only exacerbates your frustration and depression. The more you think about your past negatively, the more negative you feel about your current situation. Distortion is a trick of the Deceiver to rob you of your God Moments.

The truth is, God has never left you or forgotten you. Your life is not less blessed than other lives. Your existence is not less valuable than another person's existence. There have been marvelous moments of divine affection scattered all through your life. They may somehow have been distorted, but the real God Moments are there.

Your Father in heaven loves you—always has, always will. And whether you remember it accurately or not, He's provided for you. The pain of your life may make you feel unconnected. The failures along your journey may cause you to assume that there has been no ladder between your life and God's. But God has always been there.

Hannah had always felt abandoned by her dad. When she discovered his invisible love, everything changed. It's time for you to discover the affection of your heavenly Father. He's left a provision—not in a lockbox in a bank, but on a cross on a hill. Your Father provided by leaving you His all—His own Son, Jesus Christ. Instead of a last will and testament, He's given you His Word. You'll find your inheritance described on every page of the Bible. Instead of a lawyer to execute the will, He's given you another Counselor called the Holy Spirit. The Bible promises the Spirit will lead you into the truth.

The first reason for the Passover commandmant was that God wanted the Israelites to connect the events of the evening with His eternal purposes.

He commanded the sign of the blood for *them* so the connection would be unmistakable. You, like Jacob, may have thought you're living an ordinary earthly journey, but you are not. The message of heaven has been flying up and down an invisible ladder to your heart all along. The first keystone to harnessing your God Moments is making that connection between heaven and earth, to God's plan for your life.

Do you want to get *connected?* Start here. Acknowledge that there may be parts of your past that you are not properly remembering. Confess that the Deceiver has distorted some of your memories. If Hannah needed to revisit her sense of connection with her dad, is there a chance you need to look with fresh eyes upon your connection with your heavenly Father? Isn't it true that your pain or sin or confusion may have clouded your memory?

Maybe the old saying just isn't true.

Maybe hindsight isn't always 20/20.

CHAPTER ELEVEN

THE COMMEMORATION
KEYSTONE

Rehearsing God Moments Reactivates the Blessing

My daughter Abigail was born exactly ten weeks ago. As any honest parent will confess, a newborn brings more than joy into her parents' lives—she also brings exhaustion. The most popular greeting card we've received since her birth depicts a diapered infant and reads: *We shall not all sleep, but we shall all be changed.* That pretty much sums it up.

And the marriage, for those few weeks, just holds on. With a newborn in a bassinet next to your bed on your right and a worn-out wife who feels like a milk machine on your left, romance is relegated to the back burner—well, truth be told, chucked out the window—for days.

But this year we had a secret weapon in place to combat romance amnesia. Abby was born September 29. In October we bought tickets for the last night's performance of *The Nutcracker* ballet. Just seeing it on the calendar made us smile. It was a reminder that the no-date, no-romance, no-sleep days of new parenthood do not last forever. It was a reminder that we would one day again dress in nice clothes and dine together in a nice restaurant.

But it was so much more. That date on the calendar represented a strategic principle for faith and joy. Those tickets were powerful weapons in our marital arsenal. *The Nutcracker,* for us, harnesses the power of commemoration. Let me explain.

The Nutcracker, a Christmas favorite of many, is performed each year in Winston-Salem by the local symphony and the North Carolina School of the Arts. The Stevens Center, which hosts the ballet, is elegant and intimate—especially at Christmas—and the production is so popular that people purchase tickets well in advance.

During the first year of our marriage, while we lived in Winston-Salem, Anne introduced me to the event. Adorned in our finest, we began the evening with an exquisite dinner at Ryans Restaurant. Our table overlooked a lovely woods. Although a full meal for two at Ryans requires a second mortgage, it was worth it.

After the feast we drove downtown past the Christmas Moravian stars that hung cheerfully from the Main Street lamps. We parked the car and made our way down Cherry Street, huddling close for warmth, nervously checking coat pockets for tickets, and holding hands to cross the street.

Lights dimmed. Tchaikovsky soared. Dancers floated.

But most of all, a tradition was born.

Little did I realize that we had begun a tradition which we would live out every year of our married life. For the last fourteen years, no matter where we've been living, Anne and I have made every effort to dress in our best, feast at Ryans, and drink in the *Nutcracker* performance.

By now, it's not the dinner or the dance that's important. It's the memory.

In the first place, we've made Ryans a place for celebrations. In addition to *Nutcracker* evenings, we've eaten at Ryans for wedding anniversaries and birthdays. It was at Ryans that I gave Anne a sapphire ring—the color of our Bennett's eyes—in thanksgiving and honor of our first child. We thanked God for the miracle of a little boy given to us, and we wept. It was at Ryans, for my birthday dinner, that Anne gave me my best birthday present ever: little girl's booties that promised another baby on the way. We had been trying to conceive our second child for over a year. We thanked God for another miracle, and we wept.

So when we eat at Ryans, it's not just about lavish food. It's about lavish memories. Memories of newlywed love. Memories of miracles and of God's faithfulness.

So can you see what happened for us at Ryans last night? As candle-light flickered beneath Anne's quiet smile, words were hardly necessary. The warm light of positive memories rushed quietly into our souls and chased away the darkness of sleepless nights. The benefit of our time together was multiplied because all the strength, love, and joy of past moments in that same spot were welcomed into the present and, in a sense, relived. When we dine by those gently lit woods, we cannot help but rehearse the love we have shared over the years and the goodness of God toward us. The dinner transcends the ordinary because it involves a rehearsal of the extraordinary. The meal does much more than nourish our bodies; the powerful principle of commemoration feeds our souls.

The brisk walk after dinner to the Stevens Center is more than a chance to huddle closely to the love of my life. Our intertwined fingers symbolize interwoven lives. It's a proud statement to other pedestrians that this is my one and only—she's mine, I'm hers, and we like it that way. It's a reminder that the best defense against the cold shoulder of the world is the warm embrace of an enduring love.

When the music commenced, we weren't suspended with anticipation over the performance in front of us. But we *were* gripped with holy suspense at the blessings the year before us might bring. For us, the symbol of the ballet is that beauty continues and grows with the years of marriage.

When we returned home to find a youngster who had chosen, instead of eating or sleeping, to fuss at Nana, we were somehow unflustered. Yes, our long list of things to do was still waiting for us: diapers to be changed, bills to be paid, a house to be cleaned. But ahhhh…the stresses of daily life had been strangely calmed. One night of commemoration and the very best of our fourteen years of marriage was brought back to life.

THE POWER OF COMMEMORATION

Commemoration is the practice of rehearsing God Moments. When you rehearse your positive memories, you do more than refresh your mind; you actually reactivate the blessing. You reclaim yesterday's blessing as a treasure for today. If you will learn and practice the art of commemoration, you will unleash a God-given secret for genuine joy and explosive faith. It is an impenetrable shield of defense against despair. It is a reliable tool for building relationships.

And it is essential for following God.

Before parting the Red Sea, the Lord gave a mandate meant to keep the Hebrew people from sinking into future oceans of despair. Mark this text in your Bible and etch it on your heart. It's a keystone for God Moments: "This is a day you are to commemorate; for the generations to come you shall celebrate it as a festival to the LORD—a lasting ordinance" (Exodus 12:14).

Like all matters of special importance, the Scripture reiterates the command with repetition: "Then Moses said to the people, 'Commemorate this day, the day you came out of Egypt, out of the land of slavery, because the LORD brought you out of it with a mighty hand'" (Exodus 13:3). Over and over, God's Word emphasizes to fathers: "Commemorate...so that you will never forget." Commemoration has extraordinary power.

Think about it. If a Christmas *Nutcracker* tradition can launch new

GOD MOMENTS MEMO

THE COMMAND TO COMMEMORATE
CAME BEFORE THE GOD MOMENT!

Did you notice? When God commanded that the Israelites observe Passover, the Passover hadn't occurred yet. God commanded and explained the commemoration before He ever passed over the bloodstained doorways. Here's the model: Decide you are going to commemorate God Moments *before* they happen. If you'll decide today to commemorate tomorrow's God Moments, you'll find a lot more of God in your life.

love and affection in a marriage by the power of commemoration, what love and affection for God could be awakened in your own heart if you began commemorating God's hand in your life?

COMMEMORATION IS CELEBRATION

Like birthdays, anniversaries, and holidays, the feasts of Israel were grand celebrations. Notice the command again: "For the generations to come you shall *celebrate* it as a festival to the LORD" (Exodus 12:14, emphasis added; see also verse 17). The Hebrew root for the word rendered "celebrate" sometimes means "dance." All the festivals didn't include a prescribed dance, but they certainly required a dance of celebration in the heart. The feasts were not commanded to be a burden. They were meant to be a delight. Hebrew children would look forward to those weeks of special fun, good friends, and uninterrupted family time. The festivals were, true to their name, festive!

Of course, some of the mandated feasts had deeply sobering overtones. The Day of Atonement was a day of deep repentance, for example. But the whole context for the feasts was one of commanded celebration. The New Testament command for everyday life is likewise celebrative, only broader: "Give thanks in all circumstances" (1 Thessalonians 5:18). "Rejoice in the Lord always. I will say it again: Rejoice!" (Philippians 4:4).

God's plan is for us to celebrate His every blessing. In the celebration, we invite more blessing. In our praise, we invite God's habitation.

My wife is a woman of celebration. Anne makes life fun in our home, turning every little moment of victory into a celebration. She also seems to be real "lucky." Anne has a history of winning door prizes. In fact, people like to sit at her table because they figure they'll have a better chance of winning. In my first book, *A Chance at Childhood Again*, I tell the story of how Anne was chosen to "Come on down!" as a contestant on *The Price Is Right* game show. She won everything, including the showcase.

One day my mother asked, "Does Anne really have more exciting and interesting stuff happen to her, or does she just tell it better?" It was a perfect question—it's *the* question of life. Do some people really get all the breaks and thus have more cause for celebration? Or do some people really know how to celebrate and thus find more reasons to celebrate? I'm quite convinced it's the latter. Victories seek out the celebrative spirit. Joy looks for a jubilant heart. Songs find their way to ready singers.

The biblical principle taught by Jesus might seem a bit baffling or even unfair, but it is so true: "I tell you that to everyone who has, more will be given, but as for the one who has nothing, even what he has will be taken away" (Luke 19:26). The ones who learn to truly celebrate are the ones who will be given more cause for celebration. From my years of ministering to God's people, I must unequivocally conclude: *Real joy is not the product of better circumstances or even more victories; it is the product of a heart that has chosen to celebrate God.*

Commemoration is a celebration. Celebrate your God Moments. Let them dance in your heart. Build your praise life on God's faithfulness to you. When God touches your life, build a celebration around that moment.

COMMEMORATION REQUIRES REPETITION

Commemoration is not optional. Nor does the command to commemorate ever refer to a single, isolated celebration. Notice the description again: "Celebrate it as a festival to the LORD—a *lasting* ordinance" (Exodus 12:14, emphasis added). It is to be a "lasting ordinance for the generations to come" (Exodus 12:17). All the festivals were observed every year. That's seven feasts every year for every Hebrew man, woman, and child. If you lived to be eighty, you would celebrate 560 feasts!

Repetition is essential for memory. We see evidence of it in every area of life. The school child who repeats his ABCs. The baby who sleeps so much better after a regular nighttime ritual. The weight lifter who builds muscle through the "reps." The advertisers who place the same images in front of us over and over and over and....

I love both golf and tennis, but lately I'm not playing either sport very well. I picked up the game of golf later in life. At one point when I was playing a lot, I had fun posting some pretty good scores. But now, after quite a layoff, I step to the first tee and feel like the club is an alien hatchet in my hand. Sometimes I can't remember what a proper swing feels like— the memory of a beautiful golf swing doesn't really live in me.

But tennis is a different game for me altogether. I don't play much now, but as a kid, I played every day. Sometimes I would ride my bike to the courts and stay all day, playing as much as eight hours of tennis. I played tennis just about every day of my life from ages eight to eighteen. Now, even if I take a significant layoff from tennis, I can step onto a court and hit a pretty reasonable topspin forehand. Unlike a golf swing, the tennis stroke is etched into my memory. Some athletes call it "muscle memory." Of course, muscles don't actually remember—the brain does. But "muscle memory" means that something is so deeply established that you don't have to think about it anymore. I've hit so many forehands that I just can't forget how to do it.

God wants His people to develop a "muscle memory" of His faithfulness. If you commemorate God Moments over and over, the memory of His faithfulness will work its way into the very depths of your being. You need to have the memory so deeply established that a wilderness experience can't make you forget it. Just as I don't have to "think" to hit a forehand and you don't have to "think" to add up two plus two, the knowledge of God's goodness can become permanently embedded in our inmost being.

When I was growing up, my mother didn't lay down many rules. But when she did, she meant it. One of those few important rules was the "two blessing rule." At the end of every day—and I mean *every* day—each family member was required to recall two blessings the Lord had bestowed during the day. It might be as simple as "I really liked the spaghetti dinner." It might be as significant as "I was accepted into college today." I remember balking at the two blessing rule. "Mo-o-om, I don't *feel* like it," I would whine. "I can't think of any blessings. Do I *have* to?"

Yes, I had to. That law (which I thought my mean mom imposed frivolously) worked its way into my soul. Every night during the fourteen years of our marriage—no matter how exhausted or frustrated Anne or I might feel—we have not shut our eyes without asking each other, "What were your two blessings?" Without knowing it, my mother had taught the power of regularly rehearsing God Moments. Tonight when I put my four-year-old to bed, he'll squirm and complain and say, "D-a-a-d, I can't think of any." But then, upon my insistence, he'll eventually say, "My two blessings today were...."

Decide that you will repeatedly rehearse your God Moments. It's as though you have a mental tape recording playing in your mind at all times. Choosing to commemorate means filling up your mental tape recording with the God Moments of your life. After enough repetition, it becomes like a song that you can't get off your mind. Soon, you can't help but think about God's goodness. Soon, you can't help but expect the best for tomorrow.

COMMEMORATION NEEDS DETAILS

The old saying, "Practice makes perfect," isn't entirely true. Actually, only perfect practice makes perfect. If you practice a piano scale incorrectly a hundred times, you will only ingrain a wrong scale. If a football team practices a play incorrectly a hundred times, they may remember the play but they'll remember it incorrectly. Likewise, commemoration is not just about remembering, it's about remembering correctly.

Details are important. The commemoration is only as good as the recollection. I wouldn't bless my wife much if I came home on June 18 with a lovely anniversary gift for her. Our anniversary is May 18! Commemoration is not haphazard. It is rooted in the details of real history.

According to medical studies, the brain systematically filters out what it considers to be needless details. The memories of seemingly needless details are still collectively stored in the brain, but the brain doesn't focus on them or assign them value. One doctor explains it this way:

> Think about a rosebush. Specifically, a double tea rose, two-tone cream and magenta. What do you envision? Now think about what a photograph of the bush would record. The photo would show mostly green. When the size and volume of the flower is compared to the size of the bush with all the leaves, the flower is not a significant part. Even if it is blooming profusely, the bush is still mostly foliage. The flower would take up a very small part of the photograph. Yet it's the flower we remember, appearing bigger and more beautiful in memory than it actually is, not the whole photographic image. And of course, the photo cannot conjure up the heady aroma of a tea rose in full bloom. In other words, our brain sifts for the item of interest—the item of focus—and reduces the rest. Even if you were looking at the actual rosebush, you would not notice how many leaves it has or that some of

them are infected with a fungus unless you are a horticulturist attuned to such things.[11]

If you aren't remembering the details of God's activity in your past, you're not remembering rightly. God is in the little stuff too. Notice again how much detail is mandated in the Passover commemoration.

There were details of time:

- "on the tenth day of this month each man is to take a lamb" (Exodus 12:3);
- "take care of them until the fourteenth day of the month" (Exodus 12:6);
- "slaughter them at twilight" (Exodus 12:6);
- "Celebrate the Feast of Unleavened Bread because it was on *this very day* that I brought your divisions out of Egypt" (Exodus 12:17, emphasis added).

There were details for the feast:

- "Do not eat the meat raw…roast it…. Do not leave any of it till morning…. Eat it with your cloak tucked into your belt, your sandals on your feet and your staff in your hand" (Exodus 12:9–11);
- "For seven days no yeast is to be found in your houses" (Exodus 12:19);
- "Take a bunch of hyssop, dip it into the blood in the basin and put some of the blood on the top and on both sides of the doorframe" (Exodus 12:22).

All the feasts have very specific requirements. God Moments are not vague generalities. They are specific, real-life instances of God's activity. God commanded a precise commemoration because it would produce a precise memory.

Which is a more powerful memory: (1) "Years ago we were in a tight spot financially, but God helped us through it." Or (2) "March 13, 1994, we hit rock bottom financially. We didn't know how we would pay the overdue electric bill. Then a letter arrived from an old friend on March 14. He'd heard that I had lost my job. He enclosed a check for $150—$2 more than the amount of the electric bill."

The more specifically you commemorate your God Moments, the more powerful they will be in stengthening you for the future.

COMMEMORATION USES THE POWER OF ASSOCIATION

If you give Tatiana Cooley fifteen minutes to memorize 100 faces and names, she will easily remember at least seventy of them. Tatiana is the reigning USA National Memory Champion. She can also remember most of a list of 500 miscellaneous words: "liquid, dairy, digit, district, garden, hair...." How does she do it? By *association*. She creates a story that links otherwise random numbers and words.

Have you ever been unable to remember a name or a fact, but later had it pop into your mind because something triggered the memory? We remember things by association. We file things in our minds with all kinds of linkages. We recover memories when we learn what the event or fact is associated with.

Symbols and memorials provide tangible associations for remembering God Moments. All the feasts incorporated tangible symbols of God Moments: Blood on doorposts. Unleavened bread to eat. Firstfruits to offer. Rams' horns to trumpet. Leafy booths to live in. Old Testament saints piled rocks at the spot of the God Moment in order to link their memory with the moment. We can find reminders around us that serve the same memorial purpose. I call those reminders God Mementos. You can call them memorials, monuments, or whatever helps you remember to use them. In chapter 12 we'll explore further this powerful gift God has given to help remember our God Moments.

In my imagination, I breathe in deeply and savor the aroma of Ryans—the crab, the filet mignon, the fresh coffee. I savor the blessings Anne and I have celebrated there. I feel the glowing warmth of the fire in the back room. I feel the glow of a marriage that has endured these four-teen years. I close my eyes and feel the chill of the December evening when my bride and I walked the two blocks to the Stevens Center. I hear the symphony erupt with Tchaikovsky. And I hear my heart erupt with fresh love, joy, and hope. It's more than nostalgia. It's more than sentimentality. It's the stuff that helps my relationship with my wife grow richer each year.

That's what God wants in His relationship with you. He loves you more deeply than any husband ever loved a bride. He wants to impart more spiritual blessing than you can imagine. So He invites you to commemorate the special moments of love, intimacy, and beauty you have shared. He has taken you to more than a fine restaurant—He has taken you to a King's feast. He has bought you more than filet mignon—He has bought your redemption. He has escorted you to more than a pretty ballet—He has ushered you to the dance of abundant life.

God has put His hand in yours and clung to you forever. When you decide it's all worth reliving, you've discovered the Keystone of Commemoration.

....

CHAPTER TWELVE

THE COMMUNICATION
KEYSTONE

The World's Greatest Source of Encouragement

eople remember...
  ...10 percent of what they read
  ...20 percent of what they hear
...30 percent of what they see
...50 percent of what they see and hear
...70 percent of what they say
...90 percent of what they say as they do a related activity.[12]

God's smart. He made us. He understands how we function. So it's no surprise that the third keystone for harnessing God Moments is communication. Notice the command: "And when your children ask you, 'What does this ceremony mean to you?' *then tell them*, 'It is the Passover sacrifice to the LORD, who passed over the houses of the Israelites in Egypt'" (Exodus 12:26–27, emphasis added). The feast was designed ultimately to be a grand communication device.

In the beginning, God spoke to create the world. There is still something so life-giving and powerful about the spoken word that it virtually shapes the world around us. Hebrew fathers learned to speak blessings over their children. The tongue, James says, is the rudder of a great ship. Spiritual salvation is confirmed when you "confess with your mouth" that Jesus is Lord. In the heavenly war of Revelation, the devil is defeated "by the blood of the Lamb and by the word of their testimony" (Revelation 12:11). Over and over, the Bible teaches us that spoken words have an incredible, powerful command over how we feel and act. Teachers have long known that saying something out loud is one of the greatest memory tools in the world.

As a preacher and writer, most of my time is spent communicating. Like all communicators, I constantly search for more effective ways to impart truth and motivate people. The most compelling statistical studies prove that people are highly visual: We need to "see" something in order to remember it. I've started using pictures, photos, and notes in animated presentations on large screens to emphasize parts of what I preach. For example, while recently preaching on the prodigal son's return, I projected a copy of Rembrandt's marvelous painting, "The Prodigal." If you were to ask a parishioner if he remembers me preaching on the prodigal son, I hope he would answer yes. If you pressed a little further and asked if he could remember some specific points of the sermon, he'd probably answer no. But I wouldn't be surprised at all if he then added: "Oh yeah, that was the sermon in which he showed that Rembrandt painting. *Now* I remember."

This visual vitality is the very thing Jesus appealed to most when He taught. He didn't have video projection or Powerpoint presentation software, so He painted pictures with His words and pointed to nearby imagery for effect. When He taught the disciples about greatness in the kingdom, He put a child on His knee. I imagine Him tossing seeds in the air when He said, "A sower went out to sow...." He may have pointed to their fishing nets when He told the disciples He would make them fishers of men. Why did He teach like that? Two thousand years ago, long before any scholarly communication studies, Jesus understood that people remember something more than twice as well if they hear it *and* see it.

The feasts of Israel are communication masterpieces. In the Seder meal during Passover, the Hebrew father stands at a table full of visual reminders of the Israelites' amazing rescue from Egyptian bondage. During the meal, children will naturally ask: "Father, why are we eating this funny bread?" The patriarch then teaches: "When we were delivered from slavery, the Lord moved quickly. We left in haste. There was no time to wait for bread to rise. So we are eating unleavened bread with our meal to remind us how our relatives long ago left Egypt." Another child might take a bite of bitter herb and, as his face contorts, say, "Oooh, why do we have to eat this sour stuff?" Again the father communicates: "Our forefathers were slaves in Egypt. Their work was hard. Pharaoh was cruel. Bondage is a very bitter thing. We must never forget that God has delivered us from the sourness of slavery."

Each detail of the Passover feast—four cups, wine and water, unblemished lamb, bitter herbs, unleavened bread—is a visual symbol that helps the Hebrew father communicate the love and provision of God to his children. The Seder, like all the feasts, is not only an act of commemoration, it is an act of communication. The biblical mandate to tell others what God has done is emphasized again and again: "In days to come, when your son asks you, 'What does this mean?' say to him, 'With a mighty hand the LORD brought us out of Egypt" (Exodus 13:14). "In the future, when your son asks you, 'What is the meaning of the stipulations...?' tell him: 'We were slaves of Pharaoh in Egypt, but the LORD brought us out of Egypt with a mighty hand'" (Deuteronomy 6:20–21).

God Moments are not special secrets to be locked away in the hearts of the spiritually elite. They are public announcements of God's goodness for anyone who has ears to hear. Of course, there are times and places for sharing God Moments as the Lord leads and makes them available. We aren't called to communicate our God Moments with every person we see. But you will never fully harness the power of your God Moments until you communicate them with someone else. Communicating God Moments seals them upon your own memory, builds your faith for the future, and honors God among those who hear you. Simply put, the discovery of your God Moments is the foundation of your testimony and your witness.

GOD MOMENTS AND THE MAKING OF YOUR TESTIMONY

Not long ago, when teaching on the subject of developing a personal testimony, I decided to use the communication principle of "learn-more-by-seeing-and-hearing" in two ways.

First, I played a little trick. "I want to introduce you to my best friend. I consider him to be a special gift to me—I didn't earn his presence in my life or buy the privilege of having him. He was a free gift. He is the kind of friend who is always there. He's a shoulder to cry on—a warm presence to count on. I'm confident that he'll never leave me or forsake me. If we've been separated, it's not been his fault. I'm always the one leaving him out of my life, never vice versa. He'll let me talk to him anytime. Sometimes I just pour my heart out to him. He never grows impatient with me; he just keeps listening. He seems so real that I can actually feel his warm touch. Not everyone loves him, but I sure do. He is nothing but beautiful to me."

Several parishioners grew misty-eyed as I told of my love. When I asked them to identify my friend, they of course responded, "It's Jesus."

That's when I brought out Gus. Gus is a big, plush, ugly, stuffed animal—a fuzzy bulldog. Anne gave him to me years ago. "Nope. It's not Jesus I was talking about. It's Gus."

Amidst the rolling eyes and audible "boos," I explained. "It's all true. Every word of it. Gus was a gift. He never leaves me. He's a good shoulder to cry on. He's so real I can feel his warm touch. I do love him.

"What's missing?" I asked. "How could you have known I wasn't talking about Jesus Christ?"

My little trick worked, I think. It was plain enough for everyone to see that Gus wasn't a person. What was missing was *relationship*. A testimony is much more than a list of the attributes of God. It is not a recitation of spiritual truths. A real testimony is built upon a personal relationship with God. If you are witnessing to me, I need to hear how your life has been changed by your interaction with God in real history. I need to hear your God Moments because they are the unique markers of God's life-changing power at work in you. Just as the Hebrew fathers taught their children during the feasts, we need to tell others how we have been personally impacted, changed, and touched by God. All of your God Moments are simply stories of your growing relationship with Him. An effective testimony always builds upon a real relationship.

The second trick I used that evening was equally fun. As I read aloud the Bible passage we would be discussing, parishioner Ty Carson paraded into the fellowship hall wearing a ridiculous disguise we had scrounged up earlier. Wearing a white robe, a phony green carnation, sunglasses, and a Clemson University ball cap, Ty carried an arrangement of artificial flowers. Acting surprised, I stopped reading and stared at the strange figure who had interrupted my teaching. Others, of course, turned their heads to watch the spectacle. Per our prearranged plan, Ty handed his wife the artificial flowers, whereupon she shouted, "What are these? I didn't order these. I don't want to pay for these!"

The white-robed intruder responded loudly, "Oh, but these are free. If anyone else wants some, there are plenty more where these came from. Call me at…" and he gave out his phone number. Then Ty and his wife dashed out.

Needless to say, people were variously puzzled, amused, or disturbed. Playing it to the hilt, I picked out three random "witnesses" to interview about the event. Two stepped from the room while the first joined me at the microphone.

I asked three questions: (1) What did the man have on his head? (2) What did he give to the lady? And (3) what was the telephone number?

Amazingly, out of the three witnesses, there were only a total of two or three reasonably correct answers. In response to the first question, "What did he have on his head?" one witness replied, "Hair." None knew it was a ball cap, much less a Clemson University hat. Only one remembered that the gift to the woman was flowers, but couldn't remember the color of the phony bouquet. Only one man was able to tell me the phone number because he had figured out my little game and written it down!

The charade provided a teachable moment. Everyone witnessed the same event, but not everyone remembered the same thing. In fact, the surprising truth was that no one remembered very much about an incident that had taken place before their eyes just minutes before.

The learning activity taught me again the principle we learned in the previous chapter: that details are important. Being an effective witness begins with being a keen observer. There is so much activity around us all the time that, unless we focus and choose to remember a moment, the memory will be filed in some inaccessible compartment of the brain. If such is true of natural events, so it is of spiritual events. As I have repeatedly asserted, *the question is not whether God has been active in our lives—it is how much we have observed.* To be an effective witness for Jesus Christ, you must become committed to keen observance of His hand in your life. To establish a meaningful testimony, you must recapture the specific details of your God Moments.

THE WORLD'S GREATEST COMPLIMENT

The Communication Keystone is all about recognizing and telling others what God has done in your life. Equally important, it requires telling others *how you see God in them.*

Notice the heart and intention of the communication mandate. "Tell them, 'It is the Passover sacrifice to the LORD, who…spared *our* homes'" (Exodus 12:27, emphasis added). *Our* means "mine *and yours."* In other words, the father wasn't just reciting something that had happened in his great-great- grandparents' lives, or even in his own life—the father was sharing with his son what God had done in the *boy's* life. Thus the feast communicates an extraordinary, twofold truth: "God has been active in my life *and* God has been active in your life."

The greatest encouragement a friend can give another is, "I've really seen God at work in your life." Parents can greatly encourage their children by pointing out God Moments they witness in their children's lives.

Some months ago, our four-year-old, Bennett, was leaning back in his chair at the kitchen table. After politely but unsuccessfully asking him to refrain, I decided to provide a dramatic retelling of the time in which I, as a youngster, leaned too far back in my chair at the kitchen table. In that real-life account, the legs of the chair slipped, I catapulted backward, gashed my chin, and was rushed to the emergency room for five stitches. I assured Bennett that God was protecting me, but that the Lord still wants us to act safely. Wide-eyed Bennett was mesmerized by my story and, I must admit, has leaned back in his chair considerably less since then.

A week later, Bennett was riding in the backseat of our family car alongside his good buddy, Walker. Anne, who was driving, overheard an interesting conversation that went something like this:

Walker: "When my daddy was little, he fell off a motorcycle on the road. But God was with him and he didn't die."

Long pause.

Bennett: "When *my* daddy was little, he fell off a chair in the kitchen. But God was with him and he didn't die."

How casually others, especially children, pick up our stories!

As I have learned about the power of remembering God Moments,

I've made focused efforts to instill God Moment memories in my little boy. As I shared in an earlier chapter, Bennett recently fell off the four-foot brick wall by the driveway. Fortunately, other than a scraped leg and lots of tears, he came through unscathed. I took the opportunity to say, "Wow, God must have really been with you to keep you from being hurt worse. I wonder if an angel protected you?"

Imagine my surprised delight when, the other day, Bennett observed, "Daddy, I fell off the steps today but I didn't get hurt because God was with me. Come and let me show you where I fell." After pointing out the place where he had foolishly climbed outside the banister and fallen off the fourth step, Bennett smiled and asked, "Dad, was that a God Moment?"

Years ago I undertook a study of the life of John Wesley, the itinerant preacher who set the gospel ablaze among British coal miners with his open-air preaching in the 1700s. What was the root of the passionate call on this man who founded Methodism? Most people point to the day at Aldersgate in which his heart was "strangely warmed." Instead, I became convinced that the root of Wesley's call was a much earlier God Moment. When he was a little boy, John Wesley was trapped in his family's burning house. Just when it looked as though little John would perish, a neighbor made a miraculous rescue. Wesley's mother announced what would become a prophetic blessing over her little boy: "You are a brand plucked from the burning. God has saved you for great purposes." Suzanna Wesley instilled a God Moment in her child that may otherwise have been lost. In turn, John Wesley led a revival that touched the whole world.

Instilling God Moments in others accomplishes far more than a mere word of encouragement or flattery. When you pay a person a fine compliment ("Nice dress" or "Good job on that report you did") you make her feel good about herself momentarily. But eventually such compliments fade and the person is left hungering for more affirmation of her personal accomplishments. What I really need to know is not how great I am, but how great God is in me. If you tell me I'm so wonderful that I can do anything I put my mind to, I'll feel momentarily inflated but eventually discouraged. If you tell me that God is at work in me, I'm ready to take on any challenge or face any obstacle.

GORILLAS IN OUR MIDST

When our boy was three, I took him to the state zoo in a nearby city. It was his first trip to the zoo. Bennett had seen lots of pictures of animals. I had read him dozens of animal books. We had play-acted lions and tigers and bears. What a delight to watch him lay eyes on his first *real* lions, tigers, bears…and giraffes and monkeys, too.

Upon our arrival, Bennett naturally wanted to see the more ferocious animals first. So we began by seeking out the lions. Like all the animals at our state zoo, the lions dwell in natural habitats separated from spectators by a fence and a canyon barrier. Feeling utterly safe, little Bennett played his favorite game. Impersonating the biblical David, he took his imaginary sling and zinged an invisible stone at one of the unsuspecting lions. "Got him," he said. "I'm not scared of lions."

A little later we came to the gorilla habitat. Normally the gorillas are out amidst the trees and shrubbery. But on that day, several of the largest gorillas had plopped down right up against the thick Plexiglas window in the spectator viewing area. Fascinated and excited, I marched right up to the window. "Look, Bennett, we get to see the gorillas up close!" There they were, only inches away. While I was pointing and gawking, I suddenly noticed that Bennett was no longer next to me. He had retreated to a bench fifteen yards away.

"Bennett, don't you want to see the gorillas up close?"

"No, Daddy. I'm just gonna stay back here and look at them."

"But you can see them much better from up here. You can get right next to…" Then I understood. "Oh, Bennett, these gorillas can't hurt you."

I stepped back and sat beside him on the bench. *How can I take away his fear so he can enjoy this special opportunity to get close to a live gorilla?* I asked myself. I thought about explaining, "Bennett, that Plexiglas is quite thick and that gorilla can't get through it." But I considered how difficult it would be to explain the difference between Plexiglas and real, breakable glass. Furthermore, who said an angry gorilla couldn't fracture Plexiglas with a determined blow? I could reassure my son that he was safe as long as he was with me. But I thought better of that rationale, too. If the gorilla came after Bennett and I was my boy's only protection, well, bye-bye both of us.

Finally it occurred to me that I had only one convincing answer. Only one form of real, lasting encouragement. "Bennett, you're like David the shepherd boy. Do you remember what David said to Saul? 'God helped me kill the lion and the bear; He'll help me kill this giant, too.' Bennett, you're like David. You're no ordinary boy. I've seen God at work in you. As long as God is with you, you're safe. God is a whole lot stronger than any gorilla."

I went back to the Plexiglas and waited. Within a few minutes my little "David" crept up beside me. Together, we smiled and marveled at a gorilla only inches away.

In recent decades, psychologists have espoused the importance of instilling self-esteem in our children. But, inadvertently, we have released a dangerous humanistic message. Children know there are "gorillas" in their lives. We will all face obstacles and opponents much bigger and stronger than we are. We cannot stand up to them on our own. No matter how much we are told "You can do it, you can do it, you can!" we know that there are profound limits on our human ability. Many children grow up with a confusing dilemma: *I am told that I can face anything, but I know that I can't.* It leaves grown children either riddled with anxiety or plagued with an impostor mentality.

COMMUNICATING GOD MOMENTS: A WAY OF LIFE

The scripture tells parents not to simply report evidence of God Moments to their children, but to find ways to insure that those truths make a lasting impression. "These commandments that I give you today are to be upon your hearts. Impress them on your children. Talk about them when you sit at home and when you walk along the road, when you lie down and when you get up" (Deuteronomy 6:6–7). The word translated "impress" in the New International Version is the Hebrew verb meaning "sharpen," as one sharpens a sword or arrow. In the Deuteronomy passage, it conveys the sense of diligent, repeated teaching—like one sharpening a blade on a stone. Communicating God Moments requires consistency and frequency. To be most effective, communicating God Moments should become a way of life.

Pointing out the God Moments you see in others makes you one of God's messengers. In a recent study of angels, I noticed that the divine messengers of the Bible carry a distinct kind of message. Like the angel who called a quivering Gideon a "mighty warrior," or Gabriel reassuring a frightened teenager named Mary, the heart of the angelic message is often simply, "I've seen God at work in your life." In other words, angels communicate God Moments.

The deepest form of encouragement you can offer another human being is to share heaven's perspective of God's work in his or her life. As you cultivate the keystone of communicating God Moments to others, you share the message of angels!

*M*y wife has a godly heritage. There's never a family gathering in which some story isn't told about Mama Bennett and her knowledge of God. I love hearing the stories. When her son Stanley was spared in the jeep accident I described in an earlier chapter, Mama Bennett was simultaneously touched by the Spirit and moved to prayer. The mother's prayers uttered in South Carolina were linked to a miraculous rescue of her soldier boy in Germany. The whole family knows it.

On another occasion, Mama Bennett had a visit from a snow-white dove. After her father-in-law's death, she was restless and concerned about whether he was in heaven. One day, while praying about her concern, a dove entered her open bedroom window and landed on the bedpost. Coincidence? No way you'd convince her of that. It was all the assurance she needed—an extraordinary God Moment.

Mama Bennett never kept the miracles secret. She was a communicator of God Moments. And her testimonies have shaped Anne's spiritual heritage. After all, if you've heard your grandmother tell story after story about God's presence in your family, you start expecting God in your own life. The message is clear: *We're no ordinary family—God is at work in us! We have God in our family.*

Good news: You do, too! Practice the Keystone of Communication. Share God Moments with others. And may God provide others to communicate God Moments to you.

CHAPTER THIRTEEN

....

ROCK-SOLID
REMINDERS

Keep God Mementos to Remind You of His Blessings

IRE! FIRE! YOUR HOUSE IS ON FIRE!"
Quick, get out! Time is short! Grab only one item.
What would you take?

Ponder for a moment and really answer the question. What would be the one thing you'd want to save? Not long ago, I asked that question of a crowd. I wouldn't be surprised if you answer it the way 85 percent of those people did.

Their answer? Pictures. Some said photo albums. Some said wedding portraits. Some said childhood slides. Some said home videos. But in one form or another, most people said they would save the photographic record of their families.

Interesting, isn't it? In such a materialistic age, most people would bypass hundreds of items worth far more money to save a book of faded photos. What's so precious about pictures? We want to remember the meaningful moments of our lives, so we take pictures to remind us of the family trip to the Grand Canyon.

Still, is it really that important to keep a picture of the Grand Canyon? You can buy postcards of much better photographic quality. Sure. But you can't buy a picture of your three smiling kids standing in front of the Grand Canyon—or anywhere else. If I ask you why you like those photos of the kids standing in front of the Grand Canyon, you might just say, "It makes me feel good." What you would mean is that the photo helps you remember the moment and, in a sense, relive it. If I press you further, you may admit, "It's not really the Grand Canyon that makes me feel good—it's my three children who make me feel good. That trip was one of the best times we ever had with the kids."

The reason most of us would salvage pictures first is because in them are the people we love and who love us. Loving and being loved—that's what we want to remember because that's what life is all about.

I carry a little digital memo recorder in my pocket to keep track of names, numbers, and thoughts. Most of the stuff I record is eventually deleted, put into a computer file, or completed. But at the beginning of my "thoughts" file is a recording I hope to keep forever. In fact, if I lost the little recorder, I'd be more concerned about losing that first little recording than I would all the other memos, dates, and appointments combined.

When our little boy was two years old, we started a game almost every parent has played. We'd ask one another, "How much do you love me?" The standard but exuberant response would be uttered with a smile and arms stretched as wide as humanly possible: "I love you more than *this!*" One day I pulled out my memo recorder and recorded Bennett's two-year-old voice calling out, "Daddy, I love you more than *this!*"

Imagine the ministry that recorded memento has in my life today. When someone on the freeway doesn't like the way I entered his lane and shares his dissatisfaction with a gesture and a verbal wish for my final destination, I pull out my recorder. When I've made an unpopular decision or been falsely accused or simply mistreated, I can either dwell on how many people don't love me or I can pull out my recorder. No matter how bad a day I'm having, a little gadget in my pocket will prove to me that someone on the face of the earth loves me more than the distance of two outstretched arms.

Of course, I know that Bennett loves me even if I don't play the recording. I can use my imagination to remember the sound of his voice. I can meditate on his love even if I don't have the recorder with me. Bennett won't quit loving me because I don't have the recording. And I probably won't ever completely forget the sound of his two-year-old voice. I don't absolutely have to have that recording to remember his love. But my, how it helps!

It all makes me wonder…if we crave mementos that will remind us of special moments with people we love, why don't we keep reminders of our special moments with God? Just as the distinct memory of Bennett's voice will probably fade without a recording to remind me, our God Moments can lose their luster if we have no tangible reminders of them.

GOD'S WAY OF HELPING US REMEMBER

God Moments are of infinite value, even more so than precious photos of loved ones. They deserve tangible reminders to keep the holy memories fresh. I like to call such reminders God Mementos. But the idea certainly isn't mine—it's God's. In fact, the pages of scripture are dotted with examples of these rock-solid reminders.

When Jacob dreamed of the angelic ladder, he was overcome by the powerful God Moment. He exclaimed, "Surely the LORD is in this place, and I was not aware of it" (Genesis 28:16). As we saw in an earlier chapter, Jacob discovered that his life was invisibly intertwined with heaven. His next exclamation proved it was a God Moment of Revealed Truth: "How awesome is this place! This is none other than the house of God; this is the gate of heaven" (Genesis 28:17).

Overcome by the spiritual encounter, Jacob didn't want to forget the spot or the moment. "Early the next morning Jacob took the stone he had placed under his head and set it up as a pillar and poured oil on top of it" (Genesis 28:18). It was just an ordinary stone but it symbolized an extraordinary moment. In a similar incident, after God spoke to Jacob at Bethel, "Jacob set up a stone pillar at the place where God had talked with him" (Genesis 35:14).

In the same fashion, when God supernaturally fought for the Israelites against the Philistines at Mizpah, the prophet Samuel "took a stone and set it up between Mizpah and Shen. He named it Ebenezer, saying, 'Thus far has the LORD helped us'" (1 Samuel 7:12). Ebenezer means "stone of help." To say "thus far has the Lord helped us" is to build everyone's faith that the Lord will help us in future battles as well.

In another instance, when Moses received God's word for Israel, "He got up early the next morning and built an altar at the foot of the mountain and set up twelve stone pillars representing the twelve tribes of Israel" (Exodus 24:4). At Mount Ebal, Moses similarly instructed the people: "Keep all these commands that I give you today. When you have crossed the Jordan...set up some large stones and coat them with plaster. Write on them all the words of this law when you have crossed over" (Deuteronomy 27:1–3).

We've already seen how different it was for the Israelites to cross the parted waters of the Jordan compared to the parted Red Sea. When they crossed the Red Sea, the exuberant Israelites danced, sang, and celebrated but made no memorial—no God Memento to mark the power of the moment. Within a few days these same people were grumbling in the desert, doubting their whole deliverance. But when they crossed the Jordan years later, the Lord instructed them to have twelve men take twelve stones from the midst of the miracle and erect a memorial.

> And Joshua set up at Gilgal the twelve stones they had taken out of the Jordan. He said to the Israelites, "In the future when your descendants ask their fathers, 'What do these stones mean?' tell them, 'Israel crossed the Jordan on dry ground.' For the LORD your God dried up the Jordan before you." (Joshua 4:20–23)

We don't naturally tend to set up reminders of God's activity in our lives. In fact, it's likely that you'll find yourself amazingly distracted from the whole practice. Why didn't the Israelites make a rock pillar to commemorate the Red Sea miracle? Perhaps, in their exuberant celebration, it just never occurred to them that such a dramatic supernatural event would be possible to forget. Who could forget a Red Sea experience? When we assume that our moment with God is so powerful and passionate that it could never dim, we feel no draw toward marking the moment. But as we have seen, the searing heat of desert adversity will try to melt even the most profound God Moments into shapeless, doubtful experiences. God Mementos help us through the desert times when our memory is threatened by the dry heat of tribulation.

Maybe the Israelites didn't set up a memorial from the Red Sea because there was too much other important activity going on around them. With the celebration, the journey ahead, the directions from Moses, and a hundred other seemingly important items, it may have seemed needless to set up a pillar of rocks.

Perhaps the most obvious reason the Israelites erected no Red Sea monument was that they had no instructions regarding how to do it. They were just ignorant of the importance of such memorials. If you, like I, have felt ignorant about how to make God Mementos, think about how easy it was for the Israelites. They simply used rocks. Just plain old stones. But those rocks teach us some of the essential characteristics of God Mementos:

- Rocks are simple. God Mementos are best kept simple. They need not be expensive, fancy, or even unique as long as they clearly remind you of the God Moment.
- Rocks are immediately accessible. When an Israelite had an encounter with God, he or she didn't have to leave the area to look for the reminder. Anyone who has traveled in the Middle East can tell you there is no shortage of rocks!
- Rocks endure. When a pillar was erected, it stood a long time. Choose God Mementos that will last.

Consider also three other good lessons God's children learned about erecting memorials:

1. *They set up the memorial immediately after—or even in the midst of—the God Moment.* Have you ever awakened thinking about a vivid dream you had, but then forgot the dream a few minutes later? If an event isn't written down right away, it may become lost forever. God Mementos need that kind of immediacy. You are in a spiritual battle. The enemy cannot stop God from blessing you, so he'll try to stop you from remembering the blessing. You will face every manner of temptation to put off marking a God Moment, so take action to mark the Moment. You'll be glad for every God Memento you keep.

2. *The Israelites set up memorials that could be easily revisited.* A God Memento that's just too hard to find or visit is of little value. I used to take slide photographs. Slides are cheaper, sharper, and can be projected. But I never looked at them. Slide projectors were just too much trouble. I have a lot of great slides—somewhere! Now I just take prints. Anne is great at making creative photo albums and they're so much more accessible. Keep your God Mementos accessible so you'll revisit them often.

3. *The Israelites set up public memorials.* At least some of your God Mementos need to be shared with others. The Israelites set up rock pillars

THE GOD MOMENT PRINCIPLE

not only to remember their God Moments, but also to share with others about them. Of course, certain intimate encounters with God are too personal to share with anyone. But many of the rock-solid reminders we establish can serve as encouraging witnesses to the power and goodness of God.

KINDS OF GOD MEMENTOS

Memorabilia
Look for creative items that connect you to your God Moments.

One family in our church has a literal rock pile in their backyard. Every time a family member is significantly blessed by God, the family gathers at the rock pile and hears a brief testimony as the family member adds a rock to the pile. They can't walk through the backyard without remembering the pile of blessings God has showered on their lives.

Another Christian couple was having a difficult time financially. The husband was between jobs and their savings were depleted. They were facing the certain loss of their home when an unmarked envelope arrived with two-months' house payments inside. That money literally made the difference between keeping and losing the house. They felt certain it was from someone within their church, but they've never known for sure. The couple framed the envelope as a reminder of an unearned blessing.[13]

Kelly Barrett is our worship leader. In the midst of a hectic time in Kelly's life, the Lord revealed an important truth. Kelly saw himself carrying a stack of wood in his arms. As he walked along, others would approach him and ask, "Will you carry my wood too?" Kelly would answer, "Sure, one more piece will be all right." But in a short time the load grew heavy—Kelly was exhausted and overburdened. The Lord used that image to help Kelly realize that he wasn't responsible for all the world's problems. It saved him from the dual trap of workaholism and people-pleasing. Today, Kelly keeps a miniature woodpile on his desk to remind him to choose his priorities wisely. That woodpile is his memento to a God Moment of Revealed Truth.

Photographs
Expand your perspective of photos and videos.

When Jacob said of his God Moment at Bethel, "Surely God was in this place and I didn't know it," he grabbed a rock. However, if he'd had a camcorder handy, I'm confident that he would have captured the moment on camera instead. Photos and videos can be wonderful God Moment reminders. Anne and I have come to view photographs not just for their warmth and sentimentality, but for their deeper value as God Mementos.

We were married ten years before having our first child. After waiting so long, imagine our dismay when more than a year passed before we were able to conceive. One January day when Anne and I were at a point of real discouragement, we got together and prayed with some dear friends who also were ready to start a family. It was a special moment of passionate petition. Together, we agreed on our requests before the Lord. That month, both couples conceived. Our babies were born two weeks apart!

Similarly, I'm convinced our second child was the result of her big brother's prayer. After Anne and I had been trying to conceive for a long time, three-year-old Bennett said to us, "I want to ask God for a baby." We encouraged him to pray. The toddler went to the corner of the room and uttered a childlike prayer to God. When he walked back to us, Bennett confidently reported, "God said He's going to give us a baby right now." As best we can tell, Abby was conceived that week!

Now, when I look at their pictures, I see not only two beautiful children, I see two miracles. Every photograph can become a God Memento when you affirm the blessing of God it represents.

Journals
Write down the details of your God Moments and record your feelings.
Perhaps the greatest, most proven means of memorializing your experience of God is through the discipline of keeping a journal. In Morton Kelsey's words:

> The deep relationship with God which can be received and integrated in many men and women is limited by the amount of effort and time and discipline they will take to keep some record of their encounters with [God].... I doubt whether those who can read and write are able to come to the deep relationship with the Divine Lover, which is possible for them, if they do not keep a journal."[14]

Like rocks, pen and paper are almost always handy. And you can revisit a notebook anytime. Journaling allows you to draw a picture of your God Moment in words. Unlike other reminders, a journal is usually just for you. When God speaks to you, record those revealed truths. When you escape a dangerous predicament, write down the details of the Amazing Rescue. Record the ways in which God drew you unto Himself. Reflect on paper about the grace of God during your desert days. The act of writing itself will help seal the memories. And, even years later, a meditative rereading of your journal entries will bring the God Moments rushing back.

Once it's on paper, the God Moment is cemented with a powerful new objectivity. Once in permanent written form, the Tempter loses power to distort it. Author Madeline L'Engle said of her journaling: "If I can write things out, I can see them, and they are not trapped within my own subjectivity. I have been keeping these notebooks of thoughts...since I was about nine, and they are, I think, my free psychiatrist's couch."[15]

Think of everything we regularly write down in our society: stenographers record every word of a courtroom trial; clerks record the minutes of board meetings; doctors dictate their diagnoses and treatment plans for the charts; musicians write down their songs; journalists record the news; and the IRS—well, you get the idea. Here's the point: If we as a society write down anything and everything that seems important to remember, *why do we leave the paper blank when it comes to God Moments?*

If you don't currently keep a journal, don't be overly ambitious at first. You probably won't start by writing an hour each day. Try two or three entries a week. If a God Moment emerges when you don't have time to really reflect on it, at least record some sketchy details of the blessing. A few details will trigger enough memory later to engage in a true, spiritual meditation for your journal entry. And by the way, keep your journal private so you won't be inhibited as you write.

Another helpful form of journaling is the prayer journal. Simply record and date your prayer requests. Review the list regularly and note the blessings God provides in response to your prayers. It could become an ongoing God Moments log.

If you are approaching the final season of your life, you might want to give serious consideration to writing your spiritual autobiography to pass on to your children or friends.[16] I can't imagine a greater gift to a child than a parent's God Moment diary.

THE ULTIMATE REMINDER

Celebrating the Passover with His disciples, Jesus seized upon the power of memorials.

> While they were eating, Jesus took bread, gave thanks and broke it, and gave it to his disciples, saying, "Take and eat; this is my body." Then he took the cup, gave thanks and offered it to them, saying, "Drink from it, all of you. This is my blood of the covenant, which is poured out for many for the forgiveness of sins." (Matthew 26:26–28)

Every time Christians watch the bread rip, we are reminded of the nails tearing through the wrists and feet of our Messiah. Every time the wine is poured, we see His blood spilling upon Calvary's barren ground. Every loaf reminds us that the Bread of Life is sufficient to sustain us. Every cup reminds us that the Fruit of the Vine can abide in us. Every swallow reminds us that the true Manna came from heaven to live in us. Every sip reminds us that our hearts are made clean through our Lord Jesus Christ. More starkly, every communion celebration reminds us that Jesus experienced hell so that we would not. All of us, in Christ, are brands plucked from the burning.

Now imagine the shout again: "FIRE! FIRE! YOUR HOUSE IS ON FIRE!"

You scramble, grabbing what is precious. You sprint to the door. You look in your hands. What's there? It's not tax refunds, TVs, or toys. It's photos, journals, and memorabilia. But really, it's more than that. What have you rescued? Your story. You have treasured the trinkets that will remind you of who you are and who loves you.

Smoke alarms, sprinkler systems, and good sense will probably spare you the agony of ever hearing the words, "Your house is on fire!" But mortals who choose to walk the way of God are almost certain to face fiery darts. The threat will come from the keeper of the infernal fires who wants you to feel the scorching heat of hellish persecution. When the smoke of doubt begins to burn your spiritual eyes and your faith begins to cough and sputter, you'll probably start groping for the most valuable treasures of your spiritual life. You'll want tangible evidence of God's love. Stuff you can feel in your hands. Rock-solid reminders. You'll want God Mementos. When the fiery assault of the Adversary gets intense, you'll only want belongings that remind you to whom you belong—and of the promises that belong to you.

Decide today to mark your moments with God. You'll treasure those memorials tomorrow.

······································

CHAPTER FOURTEEN

"NOTHING...BUT THE BLOOD"

*Drawing Power and Peace from
Your Ultimate God Moment*

The central symbol of Christianity is the cross. It is foolishness to the modern mind, a stumbling block to the Jews, and it is even becoming lost in our society despite polls that show that 80 percent of Americans claim to be Christians.

However, we will never grasp the wonder of the gospel or apprehend its power for our lives until we encounter our Lord Jesus hanging on a Roman timber, bleeding, and slowly suffocating. The cross is our most important God Moment. None of our other God Moments will make sense or hold power until we watch the blood flow down from Calvary and marvel at the cleansing, saving power of the cross of Jesus Christ.

The cross is also essential for God Moments because it is prefigured in the Passover. As we have seen throughout these pages, the Passover in Egypt was the foundational God Moment for the Hebrew people. The Passover's message was all-important then—and now.

So please join me for a journey back 3,500 years to ancient Egypt on the night of the Passover. If you'll allow your imagination to transport you with me, you will encounter one of the most harrowing sights you've ever beheld—followed by the most glorious revelation you could ever witness.

It seems an ordinary day in the Egyptian village. Merchants are selling their wares. Mothers are feeding their babies. Children are playing ball in alleyways. However, as you eavesdrop on mundane conversations, you pick up clues that life has not been ordinary in Egypt lately.

You hear people talking of strange happenings in their land. Bizarre phenomena—hordes of frogs jumping from the Nile, swarms of locusts descending upon the fields, unusual hail storms, eclipses of the sun. Some citizens quietly mutter that it's all because of the Hebrew slaves. Others are proudly defiant. You overhear one Egyptian official scoffing: "We are the greatest civilization on earth. Ha! These so-called plagues haven't stopped us. Everything is back to normal now. Eat, drink, and be merry, everyone! Egypt is safe."

But Egypt has never been more *unsafe*.

It is the fourteenth day of the first month in the Hebrew calendar. As dusk approaches, you find a hiding place near a residential street corner and wait to observe the horror and the glory of the evening ahead. *Shhh.* Quiet. Watch and listen. Hear the Egyptian mothers call their children in for dinner. Watch the merchants close their shops. Watch the Hebrew families return to their humble slave-labor houses.

Then you're puzzled by a strange sight. It's just after twilight when you notice a Hebrew father quietly creeping to the front of his house. He holds a bowl in his hands. He glances to his right, to his left, then back over his shoulder. Hastily, he brushes red marks above his door and on the door posts, then slides silently back into his home. Just as you are watching him retreat, another Jewish man steps to his own front porch with a basin. He, too, paints crimson splotches. One after the other, up and down the street, Hebrew patriarchs paint strange marks around their entryways.

Baffled, you tiptoe to the first man's door for a closer look at the paint. It looks like…could it be? Blood? Reach up, feel it between your fingers. It is! Blood! Does this strange ritual foretell the events ahead? Under the cover of darkness you return to your corner hiding place and wait.

Lights are slowly snuffed in both Egyptian and Hebrew homes. All becomes dark.

Then, to your left, you hear an unknown sound. Is it the sound of horses and chariots far away? The sound creeps closer but does not get louder. It is not the rumbling of horses and chariots. It brings to mind the beating of a thousand bats' wings, but it is a lower, more subtle sound than that. It is a sound you have not heard before. If darkness had a sound, this would be its tone. If death had a voice, this would be its cadence. The sound is coming closer.

And then you see its source. How is it possible for a shadow to form in the midst of a moon-eclipsed night? You tremble to behold a darkness darker than the night. The shadow and its sound slowly shroud the street.

As the shadow licks at Egyptian homes, horrible shrieks of terror pierce the night air. "My baby! My baby!" an Egyptian mother screams. "My baby is dead—what is happening to us? Oh, help me, somebody help me!"

But there is no one to help the horrified Egyptian mother. Brothers and sisters and friends all begin pouring out of their Egyptian homes in similar anguish. "My son, my only son," a father cries out. "Oh, I've lost my only son!"

Not just children have died. *All* firstborns. A newlywed wife shrieks, "My groom, oh my beloved, wake up, wake up! Somebody help us!"

Together the people cry out: "What have we done? What has caused this? What can we do?"

Another grieving mother lifts her baby from his deathbed, then lifts her voice against the shadow's heart. "What can deliver us from this darkness?"

A voice emerges from the shadow. It resonates with authority. Like a voice of eternal power, rolling down through the ages and down this Egyptian street, the voice answers the woman's desperate question. "Nothing." The awesome voice pauses, then continues. "Nothing can deliver you." Then more deliberately it thunders: "Nothing...but the blood."

You watch in horror as you notice a familiar Egyptian man scramble frantically from his house toward the shadow that would soon engulf his family. You recognize this man because earlier that afternoon you noticed how kind he was. He was not like the other slave masters. This was a decent Egyptian man. He didn't beat his servants or belittle them. In fact, he sought to do all he could for them. On one occasion, at great personal risk, he issued a letter to Pharaoh calling upon the leader to end the merciless "bricks without straw" edict that had been imposed upon Hebrew slaves. He was a fine, moral Egyptian. Surely the shadow would pass over his home.

The moral man pled with the darkness. "I am a good man. I am not like my Egyptian brothers. I care for those under my charge. I am trying to bring about labor reform in the empire. Look—look here!" The good man unfurled a scroll listing his humanitarian accomplishments and validating his acts of kindness toward the Hebrews. "Look at this list," he cried. "Surely you will pass over my home!" But the darkness darker than night crept closer, undeterred, and shrouded the good man's house.

As his home was engulfed by the shadow of death, the desperate man cried out: "What then? What then? If this list and my moral standing cannot deliver me, what can deliver me from this terror?"

The voice responded, "Nothing can deliver you. Nothing...but the blood."

Another home. A woman runs out the door. She has her only son in her arms. A beautiful baby. You see the grief on her face. You pity her. You couldn't know her whole story—one of miscarriage after miscarriage— but you can see the pain etched into her brow.

She calls out in frenzy. "This baby is my only son. My only son! All the years of pain and now I am finally blessed with this baby boy. Oh, have you no pity? Surely you can have mercy upon me!"

But her home, too, is swallowed by the shadow. "If you will not pity me, what then? What can deliver me?"

Down from the ages and through the alleyway, the mighty voice shakes the night again: "Nothing. Nothing...but the blood."

You can hardly bear to watch, but another Egyptian crawls out his front door. He is the most religious man in the hamlet. He bows before the shadow and prays, "I am a devout and religious man. I am an observer of all that the gods teach. I even believe in the God of the Hebrews. Please, I pray, pass over my home because I am a devout man and I believe in God."

Unmoved by the man's religiosity, undeterred by his devotion, the shadow encroaches. As the darkness overtakes him, the religious man cries out like the others: "What then? If not my devout religious life, what can deliver me?"

Down through the ages and down the alleyway rolls the voice: "Nothing. Nothing...but the blood."

NOTHING ... BUT THE BLOOD

*A*ll is silent for a moment. Still trembling, you gather your thoughts, wipe the sweat from your brow and turn your attention to the Hebrew homes. The Jewish slave quarters are just down the street. They are next. Slowly the shadow moves toward the first of the Hebrew houses. You can't decide whether to cover your ears or cover your heart.

A special horror strikes you because you recognize the first home. Earlier that day you overheard a fight in the family. There had been terrible turmoil. The stress of the slavery, the bricks without straw, and the repeated beatings had built to rage within a Hebrew boy. The adolescent had done the unthinkable earlier that day—he had raised his voice and cursed his mother. The boy's father had unleashed his own pent-up wrath and had whipped his son mercilessly. The children had screamed. The home was filled with blasphemy and cursing. You had heard it all. And now the brutal darkness approaches the seething, blasphemous household.

Inside, the family is huddled together. They know the sins of the day and the events of the night. The shadow approaches undaunted, undeterred. But something strange happens. A marvelous, mysterious twist. As the shadow's first tendrils touch the door posts, the darkness backs away from the home. Instead, a glorious, pleasant light sweeps into the living room of the frightened Hebrew family.

They look at one another and shout, "We're alive! We're alive! It passed over us. The darkness passed over our home!" They begin to celebrate and dance with joy. Then, abruptly, they stop and begin to weep.

The boy who had cursed his mother weeps loudest. Finally he asks, "But Daddy, how could it be? Why was I spared? Daddy, what did we do to deserve this mercy? Why us? After all we've done? Daddy, what do we have that others don't?"

The Hebrew patriarch reflects on his own despicable wrath, chokes back his sobs, raises his head and slowly answers. "Nothing, son. We did nothing. We have nothing." Then he points his hand toward the front door. "Nothing...but the blood."

Another Hebrew home, this one full of sickness. The parents are aging, the children infirmed. They have been disabled by the Egyptian beatings. They are hanging on to life—merely existing—totally unproductive. You watch this home in which the least of the least huddle together in the middle of their living room. Their lives hang only by a thread as the shadow approaches their little house.

The darkness approaches, licks at the doorposts, and then *whoosh*—passes over. As cool light streams under the doorway and fills the humble home, the family beholds one another's gaunt faces and frail hands. Finally the grandmother's voice quivers, "Why are we—the least of the Hebrews, no longer any good to the world—why are we spared? What did we do to deserve this blessing?"

The worn-out father wipes a tear. "Nothing. We did nothing. Nothing...but the blood."

Another Jewish home. A worried mother watches her only son. He has had a fever for five nights. If the fever doesn't break soon, the boy will surely die. Oh, what perilous night of agony is this? People are dying all over. If this night be filled with some dark chill, then this would likely be the night of the boy's death. So the anxious mother waits by her boy's bed and mops his brow with a cool cloth.

The shadow approaches, touches the doorposts, and moves on. As it passes over, the light passes through. The glorious stream of cool light enters the boy's room and covers him gently. Instantly his fever breaks and he awakens and asks for food. The mother weeps. The father rushes in.

"What has happened?" the father cries out with joy. "What did you do for him? How has he been delivered? What remedy did you have?"

The mother hugs her boy and sobs with gratitude. "Nothing. I did nothing. We had nothing. Nothing...but the blood."

*D*o you see it?

To say "Nothing but the blood" is also to say "Nothing *in addition to* the blood." It means that while nothing *but* the blood could save them, nothing *more than* the blood was required to deliver them.

The Passover is not a story of how God excluded the Egyptians. It is a story of how God delivered the Hebrews. It is not a story of how God punished a people who deserved something better. It is a story of how God rescued a people who couldn't have done it for themselves.

Though it all takes place 1500 years before His birth, it is the story of Jesus.

Though the gospel message is simple, most people miss it. As part of a rebellious, sin-filled world, every human being is headed for death. Feeling the inward ache or even impending doom, people cry out: "What can deliver me?" They try it all. Good works. Education. Pity. Even religious devotion. But none of it has saving power. Nothing delivers us from our sin but the cross.

Christians are simply people who have discovered the saving power of the blood that flowed from that cross and have accepted it.

When the darkness of discouragement approaches a Christian and taunts, "Who do you think you are? Why do you think you're worth anything? Don't you know how many times you've failed? What makes you think you'll make it now?" the believer smiles and answers simply: "I have no reason to think I'll make it. I have nothing. Nothing...but the blood of Jesus."

When the blackness of fear surrounds a Christian and threatens, "How do you think you'll survive? What makes you think your God even hears your prayers? What defense do you have to keep the talons and fangs of destruction from sinking into your life?" the Christian answers simply: "I have no defense. I have nothing. Nothing...but the blood of Jesus."

When the shadow of sin entices a Christian, "What avenue of escape do you have? What makes you think you'll ever avoid sin's snare? What makes you think you'll ever be free of your addiction? What do you have to deliver you from the same old besetting habits?" the Christian answers: "I have nothing. Nothing...but the blood of Jesus."

The bad news is that nothing you have done, or ever could do, will make God love you more than He loves you right now. The good news is that nothing you have done, or ever could do, is necessary to make God love you. He loves you so much that He became a man. The God-man, Jesus Christ, hung on Calvary's cross so that the darkness would pass over you at the sight of the blood.

If you've never understood this simple truth, or if you've never applied it to your life, I urge you to embrace its transforming power right now. Don't endure spiritual weakness or defeat a moment longer. Use these words to guide your own prayer to the heavenly Father:

Lord, thank You for loving me even though I don't deserve it. I believe that Jesus Christ is the Son of God and that He has died for me. By faith, I apply the blood of Jesus over my life and I accept salvation through Him. I want You to be my Lord and I want to follow You to freedom all the days of my life. In Jesus' name, Amen.

If you never remember any other divine event, you have this one incredible God Moment to cling to: Jesus on a cross—*for you*. Wonderful as all the other God Moments are, the whole of your hope is here. Jesus shedding His blood for you is the quintessential God Moment of your life and of all human history.

So if you ever become forgetful and start lapsing into spiritual amnesia, remember the cross. Sure, I hope someone hears that you were blessed by this book. I hope people ask what you "got out of it" and that you can give them a chapter-by-chapter synopsis from memory. But if you draw a blank, it would suit me just fine if you simply answer: "Nothing. I got nothing. Nothing…but the blood of Jesus."

If you say that, you've said it all.

AUTHOR'S NOTE

My beloved sister-in-law, Mary, to whom this book is dedicated, went to be with the Lord Monday, August 9, 1999. She entered the hospital emergency room the previous afternoon. Not thinking her near death, I wanted to encourage her during her hospital stay, so I showed her the dedication of *The God Moment Principle* instead of waiting to give it to her on her birthday, which would have been the following week. Mary smiled tenderly, looked me deeply in the eyes, and told me she loved me. It was worth writing the book for that moment—a God Moment because I never could have known it would be my last such conversation with her.

NOTES

1. Kim Underwood, *The Winston-Salem Journal*, 18 February 1999.

2. Charles H. Spurgeon, *Morning and Evening* (USA: Hendrickson Publishers, 1991), 382.

3. Greg Asimakoupoulos, "Illustrations," *Leadership*, vol. 16, no. 4.

4. Henri Nouwen, *The Return of the Prodigal Son* (New York: Image Books, Doubleday, 1994), 35.

5. This insight and others regarding the parallel between Sinai and the first-century Pentecost are derived from the video teaching resource, "The Feasts of Israel." Karl Coke Evangelistic Association, Charlotte, NC.

6. Daniel Goleman, *Emotional Intelligence* (New York: Bantam Books, 1997), 81. The study quoted took place on the Stanford University campus and was conducted by psychologist Walter Mischel.

7. Mitch and Zhava Glaser, *The Fall Feasts of Israel* (Chicago: Moody Press, 1987), 196.

8. Jim Bakker, *I Was Wrong* (Nashville: Thomas Nelson Publishers, 1996), 373.

9. Frank Minirth, M.D., *The Power of Memories: How to Use them to Improve Your Health and Well-Being* (Nashville: Thomas Nelson Publishers, 1995), 34.

10. *The Power of Memories*, 35.

11. *The Power of Memories*, 22–23.

12. Bert Decker, "It's Not Some Mysterious Art," *Contact Quarterly,* vol. 56, no. 1, Winter 1997 (Christian Business Men's Committee of USA), 16.

13. John Trent, *LifeMapping* (Colorado Springs, Colorado: Focus on the Family Publishing, 1994), 240.

14. Bob Benson and Michael W. Benson, *Disciplines for the Inner Life* (Waco, Texas: Word Books, 1985), 99.

15. *Disciplines for the Inner Life*, 98.

16. Richard Morgan's *Remembering Your Story: A Guide to Spiritual Autobiography* (Nashville: Upper Room Books, 1996). This is a helpful tool.